THE VANCOUVER ISLAND TRAVELER

Great Adventures on Canada's West Rim

HAIDA RAVEN

By Sandy Bryson

Windham Bay Press
Juneau, Alaska

DEDICATING
this edition to
Larry Kuhl
who fished it
&
the people
who shared
Vancouver Island.

Also from Windham Bay Press:
Alaska's Inside Passage Traveler, by Ellen Searby.
The Costa Rica Traveler, by Ellen Searby.

Front cover: **Killer Whales Spyhopping** by Sandy Bryson.
Back cover: **Haida Killer Whale** by Clarence Mills.
Title page: **Haida Raven** by Clarence Mills.

All photos by Sandy Bryson unless noted otherwise.
Maps by Ellen Searby and Henry Jori.

Publisher: Windham Bay Press, Box 34283, Juneau, Alaska 99803

CONTENTS

Steve Clement ©

Bald Eagle, by Steve Clement

INTRODUCTION
to the
Vancouver Island Adventure

Orca! Killer whales approach us, blowing "KWOOF" as they swim through Johnstone Strait. David Towers tells me to climb over the side into the 6' green dinghy. I hesitate leaving the security of *Tuan*'s 43' platform to get into the bobbing boat while wearing two thousand dollars worth of camera gear around my neck. Looking out over the water, I see the tall vertical fin of a male orca paired with the rounder, shorter fin of a female coming toward us ... fast. I get in.

Shoving away from the graceful sailboat, trying to brace against the craft's rocking and rolling, I feel trapped and distorted. I have little control over what direction I can aim the cameras because a quick move will dump me into the water. Where is my dive gear? The underwater camera? Where in fact is man compared with the perfect curved lines, the awesome physical and mental power of the oncoming whales?

The whales surround my little boat. They are moving by in beautiful rhythm--blowing, diving, blowing, diving. Two youngsters spyhop a couple of meters behind me (people on the sailboat give warning yells thinking the orcas will swamp me...what could I do?), and I look one of them in the eye. Light glistens off his shiny black head. He slides back into the sea and is gone with his pod. I'm out of my depth, but I'm home free. The whales move on toward Robson Bight.

*****

Whales are the ultimate Vancouver Island Travelers. Grays on the West Coast, killers on the north side in Johnstone Strait and around the entire Island, a few minkes--the whales travel rapidly, efficiently, intelligently, without any bags or vehicles.

Introduction

All they need is the clean, free environment that really defines the islands of the Pacific Northwest: **water**. Vancouver Island is *about* water--freefalling snow, ice carving the mountains, streams rushing down their sides and watering the green forests, water drilling out the cave formations, water surrounding the Island and creating the ecological edges in which life grows.

Vancouver Island, the largest island in the eastern Pacific, lies west of Vancouver, parallel to the main coast of British Columbia in the shape of a sea mammal 450 km long and averaging 100 km wide (32,137 sq km). The spine of the Island is a range of granite peaks and alpine glaciers that rise to the highest peaks, Golden Hinde (2188 m) and Elkhorn Mountain (2179 m) in Strathcona Park, and Victoria Peak (2150 m) south of Schoen Lake Park. Eighty percent of this land stands above 150 m. The west coast fjords are as spectacular as those of Norway, Chile, or New Zealand.

Such dramatic geography directly in the path of the warm Japanese Current generates a temperate Island climate and many different life zones. Protected by the sea and the Insular Mountains, **Victoria** has the mildest climate in Canada, very similar to San Francisco in California. Average temperatures:

August = 17° C (63° F)
January = 5° C (41° F).

Victoria has 69 cm average annual precipitation, mostly as rain, and averages 6 hours of sunshine per day.

Contrast conditions on the Island's **west** coast, which gets the full force of Pacific storms. From the Victoria weather office of Environment Canada for 30 years of readings at **Tofino**, average temperatures: August = 14.4° C (58° F)

January = 3.8° C (39° F).

Yearly precipitation (primarily rain; snow at higher elevations): 254 cm. Henderson Lake, near the northeast corner of Barkley Sound, records the wettest readings in North America, 655 cm.

Watching eagles and gray whales, Calmus Passage, Tofino.

Don't let the rain stop you. First, the annual temperatures for Vancouver Island are mild. Average temperatures on the coasts are well above freezing. Second, while rain gear is standard equipment for life on the west coast, sunny days there are the clearest, most beautiful experience in the world (I have seen many of them). In defense of Island rain, it makes the trees and flowers grow, and it never bores you. Best of all for the traveler, the east side of the Island, as dry and sunny as the continental interior, is just a short drive over the hill. If you are wet in Ucluelet, you can have sunshine on Qualicum Beach in a couple of hours. After soaking in the mists and mineral waters of Hot Springs Cove, you can fish the same day under blue skies off Campbell River.

The topography and weather produce rich intertidal life (anemones, coral, sponges, sea stars, clams, crabs, shrimp, small fish), diverse forests (hemlock, willow, balsam fir, arbutus, red and yellow cedar, broadleaf maple, Douglas fir over 70 m tall, oak), giant ferns in the rainforest, wildflowers in the uplands, butterflies, and wildlife ranging from black-tailed deer, Roosevelt Elk, bear, cougar, wolves, the threatened Vancouver Island Marmot, ducks, geese, and bald eagles to trout, salmon, sea lions, dolphins, and whales.

The best economic future for Vancouver Island lies in well managed tourism. Currently, the main industries besides tourism include forest products, commercial fisheries (salmon, herring), and mining (copper, zinc, silver, iron). Research, electronics, fish farming and cottage industries are healthy and growing on the Island. The land is not suitable for agriculture except on the coastal plain of the Comox Valley that raises some grains and fruits, and small farms on the Saanich Peninsula. North Islanders, whose children are used to seeing killer whales, bald eagles and deer, like to joke about bringing animals into the classrooms to educate the students about "exotic" species they rarely see--cows, pigs, and sheep!

The permanent population of a little over 500,000 people concentrates on the eastern seaboard, with Victoria, the provincial capital, over 250,000, and Nanaimo, the second largest city, at 50,000. Considering the small size of the other east coast towns, very few people live on the large interior or west coast of Vancouver Island, an exciting concept for backcountry explorers.

HOW TO USE THIS BOOK

Adventure Section: The *Traveler* targets what **you** want to do on Vancouver Island, getting you right into these subjects. Here is all the information you need to plan a trip your way.

Your age doesn't matter. Men and women over 70 as well as teenagers are doing to some degree everything listed. Kids are flying airplanes, diving and golfing. One backcountry guide I talked to couldn't get over meeting a group of retirees bicycling back to Port Hardy from a day trip out to Holberg. Eighty-four kilometers of rough logging road...on tour bikes! There they were, bumping and jolting along, laughing and having the time of their lives. The guide just shook his head and grinned. Nobody had told them they were supposed to have flat tires or wrecks or feel rotten. So they didn't!

Whether you want to hike out to Cape Scott, sit quietly on the doorstep of your RV and watch wildlife, or dine in luxury and see a play in Victoria, the possibilities are only limited by your imagination, time and money. For me the best example is a young Islander I met who runs his own company, boardsails, waterskis, trains a dog, hikes...and is blind.

The skilled men and women who helped my research are in this book, telling you first-hand about their experiences. They are the Island's experts. They live here. I deeply appreciate their contributions.

There are some sports I have not covered in the *Traveler*. Hunting, for example. From the standpoint of pressure on some Island species and out of respect for local interests, I don't recommend visitors making a trip here specifically to hunt birds or large game. However, guides and outfitters are

Carillon Tower in Heritage Court, a Centennial gift from Holland. Wildflowers found across British Columbia bloom here.

available out of Port McNeill on the North Island for fall hunting of deer, elk, and bear.

If you can't find an activity, look under Events (Bathtub Racing, Devonshire Tea). If there's something fun to do on Vancouver Island that you don't find in this book, please write me about it. Maybe I can put it in the next edition. Any other useful suggestions or criticisms are welcome too.

Travel Section: All the important information you need to know about arriving by air or sea and getting around the Island safely and conveniently is in the Chapter 16, Tourist Information. A list of Hotels, Motels, Inns, Bed & Breakfasts, Tent and RV Campgounds appears in Chapter 17 for your convenience.

The "Good Reading" recommended in Chaper 18 is well worth your time, especially in your field of interest. As a writer and photographer, I don't say this casually: several of these books will be in my hands again and again.

Chapter 19, Maps, is at the end of the line where you can find it when you need it most. Usually that's when your partner, who is driving, screams,"Quick, here comes the intersection, which way do I turn?"

The Vancouver Island Map is designed to complement the guide's text and act as a lead-in to the specialized maps (e.g. topographic for hiking, marine charts, detailed forestry and logging road maps) you have to get for any backcountry adventures. Island cities and towns all have excellent, detailed maps featuring attractions in each local area.

I have never found Grumpy, of Seven Dwarf fame, on Vancouver Island. Even at the height of the tourist season in August, even in the busiest places, Islanders have given me only graciousness, smiles, and their valuable time. My friends report the same experiences. My only regret about visiting the Island is leaving.

Enjoy your trip to Vancouver Island. I wish you whales.

The start of an Eskimo roll? You can have all the excitement you want on Vancouver Island. (Russ Hellard, courtesy Strathcona Lodge)

Or you can take it easy.

Don Schulz climbs Port McNeill's "spar tree flagpole" to run up the flag after logger sports day in June. (Annemarie Koch)

1. EXCITING PEOPLE, PLACES, & EVENTS

A brief listing of celebrations here shows that you should contact the Tourism Association of Vancouver Island or local Travel Infocentres (Ch16) as soon as you have selected travel dates. Their complete calendars show hundreds of events and attractions, and they will send you current details free of charge.

Typical Calendar of Events

Jan _ _ _ _ _ _ _ Victoria--Art Gallery Special Exhibit
Sooke--Highlanders Pipe Band Burns Night
Comox Valley--Winter Carnival
Feb _ _ _ _ _ _ _ Nanaimo--Curling Championship
Victoria--Pacific Opera
Mar-Apr _ _ _ Victoria--Museums & Art Gallery Exhibits
Sooke--Arts & Crafts Easter Show
Jun _ _ _ _ _ _ _ Colwood--Gllangcolme Days
Gold River/Tahsis--The Great Walk, 52.5km
Victoria--Oak Bay Tea Party
Port McNeill--Logger Sports Day
Port Alberni--Strawberry Extravaganza, Rollin Art Centre
Parksville--Kite Flying Festival & Model AirShow
Victoria--Royal Victorian Rowing Regatta
Nanaimo--Shell Salute to Summer Beachparty
Sidney--Jazz Festival
Nanaimo--Pacific Rim Quarter Horse Circuit
Ucluelet/Long Beach Airport--Long Beach Fly-In
Jul _ _ _ _ _ _ _ Galiano--North Island Jamboree
Lake Cowichan--Lake Days: Logger Sports, Canoe & Raft Races
Campbell River--Salmon Festival
Nanaimo--Shakespeare Plus Festival & Bathtub Race
Port Hardy--Legion Fishing Derby
Sooke--All Sooke Day & Fine Arts Juried Show
Victoria--International Music Festival
Comox Valley--Tri-K Triathlon & Air Show

13

Courtenay--Youth Music Festival
Coombs--Blue Grass Festival
Aug _ _ _ _ _ _ Ladysmith--Dogwood Days Celebration
Ucluelet--Ukee Days
Port Hardy--Filomi Days Fishing Derby
Victoria--Oriental Exhibition, Crystal Garden
Port Hardy--Seven Hills Open Golf Tournament
Courtenay--Native Art Show
Campbell River--Raft Race & Tyee Spit
Alert Bay--Sea Festival & Salmon BBQ

Victoria--1850's Picnic at Craigflower House
Heritage Site
Victoria--Pacific Northwest Flower Show
Sep _ _ _ _ _ _ _ Victoria--Classic Boat Festival
Port Alberni--Salmon Festival
Saanich--Fall Fair
Cowichan--Exhibition
Port Alice--Fall Fair
Duncan--Exhibition
Parksville--Fantasy Auction
Campbell River--Rotary Octoberfest
Victoria--Art Gallery Special Exhibit
Comox--Octoberfest Walk
Nov _ _ _ _ _ _ Start of Christmas Fairs & Festivals Island-wide
Ski Areas Open
Dec _ _ _ _ _ _ _ Christmas Season
Nanaimo--Polar Bear Swim

Not included are **many** Loggers Sports Celebrations, Salmon Derbies & Festivals, Art & Music Celebrations all over Vancouver and the Gulf Islands.

Alert Bay

Gator Gardens-Exotic swamp-like park on top of Cormorant Island, boardwalks provide access for active person in wheelchair with help, outstanding views of Johnstone Strait & Vancouver Island, best if hosted by Alderwoman Maxine Williams

Killer whales at Sealand.

World's Tallest Totem Pole, 173'
Anglican Church over 100 years old
U'mista Cultural Centre & Nimpkish Indian Reserve
Home of Killer Whale

Bamfield

Marine Science & Research Station
Robertson Creek Hatchery
Ohiat Indian Band-Campground at Pachena Bay

Campbell River/Quadra Island

Quadra Island-Petroglyphs, beachcombing for large glass balls, shells & driftwood, oysters & clams, Rebecca Spit, Provincial Marine Park

15

Elk Falls Park & Mill-Canyon falls & dam, stand of virgin Douglas Firs, picnic area, tours

Miracle Beach Park-Nature house, salt water swimming, marine life, camping

Quinsam River Salmon Hatchery-Audio-visual displays & BBQ's

Scuba Diving-Crystal waters, wolf eels, octopus

Tyee Club-Canada's oldest Tyee Fishing Club

Skiing-Mt. Washington & Forbidden

Cape Mudge Museum-Kwakiutl Indian Band Museum

Campbell River Museum-Indian Artifacts & early history collections

Ripple Rock Lookout-Panoramic view of Seymour Narrows, site of world's largest non-nuclear explosion to remove boat-sinking rocks in Narrows

Bush Pilot Adventure Tours-Scenic tours over mountains, landing on glaciers

Chemainus Festival of Murals

Unique little town with old donkey engines, steam locomotives, loggers, seamen, and 16 larger-than-life murals telling its proud past

Cowichan River Valley & Lake Cowichan

Sarah Modeste's woolen mill where the famous Cowichan Sweaters are knit. Here the wool is carefully chosen, carded, washed, and spun into yarn. More than 125 Native women take it home to knit sweaters, toques, vests, ponchoes and socks--all by hand. 35-50 completed sweaters come back to the Modest Mill every day to be sold there and shipped to many parts of the world. Come see this craft plus more Native baskets, jewelry, totems, carvings, and leatherwork.

Kaatza Historical Museum

Lake Cowichan Satellite Earth Station-Video tape

Wildflowers of Honeymoon Bay-World's largest reserve of pink fawn lilies carpets forest floor in springtime

16

Duncan

City of Totems-Traditions totems carved by Cowichan Indian Band

Nanaimo

Shakespeare Festival-Summertime
Newcastle Island Provincial Park
Pacific Biological Research Station
Noted for Shopping Malls-6 right on the highway
Annual Nanaimo to Vancouver International Bathtub Race-Sponsored by the Loyal Nanaimo Bathtub Society attracts tubbers from Florida to Hawaii, Ilinois to Australia. All entrants receive a golden plug!

Departure Bay-Water sports and great photography

Bastion 'Noon gun' firing ceremony-All summer, 'blast from the past'

The Bastion-Fort built for protection against Indian tribes, used mainly for firing salutes, housed Hudson's Bay Company store, later became local jail, now a museum

Petroglyph Park-Northwest Coast rock carvings, underwater at high tide: Has the sea risen above ancient sea levels when these

Gunfiring ceremony, noon, Nanaimo.

17

these were carved, or were these put below water level as messages to spawning salmon? Or were they for sun-worshipping ceremonies?

Parksville

Hamilton Bird & Swamp Sanctuary-Abundant waterfowl, flora & fauna

Rathtrevor Provincial Park-Sandy swimming beach, warmest ocean swimming in B.C.,150 species birds

Coombs Market-Goats on the roof

Coombs Market.

Port Alberni

Cathedral Grove-In MacMillan Provincial Park

Robertson Creek Fish Hatchery

Holford Bay-Chinook fishing

Cameron, Sproat & Great Central Lakes-Water skiing, fishing, hiking

Diving Charters

Home of *M.V. Lady Rose*-Built in Scotland in 1937, daily runs to west coast

Stamp Falls Provincial Park

Harbour Quay-Public Market & Pier

Mt. Arrowsmith Ski Area-Summer hiking area, Winter downhill & Crosscountry Skiing

"Martin Mars" water bombers-Operated by Forest Industries Flying Tankers, recorded in the Guiness Book of Records, now on active duty fighting B.C. forest fires, tours by request

Folkfest-Do you know a perogy from a hamburger?

Port Hardy

Carrot Park-"Welcome to Port Hardy"

Cape Scott Park-Port Hardy is last stop for supplies before hike

Kwakiutl Native Arts & Crafts

Devil's Bath, Vanishing River, Eternal Fountain-Geologic sites

Quatse River Hatchery

Fort Rupert

Whaling Station at Coal Harbour

"World's Largest Burl," Port McNeill.

Port McNeill

World's Largest Burl-Weighs 22.5 tons (How did they weigh it?) & dwarfs everybody who stands by it for photos
Little Huston Lake Cave Park-Tours
Nimpkish Island Tall Trees-Tours
Ferry Dock-To Sointula & Alert Bay

Port Renfrew

Botanical Beach--In Botany Bay, a twisting drive & short hike to extraordinary tidepools, miles of natural aquariums filled with intertidal life, up to 150 m wide, full of potholes at low tide

Qualicum Beach

Horseback Riding
Golfing
Beachwalking & Swimming

Sayward

Link & Pin Museum-Antique logging equipment & tales, including a huge wooden logger named "Snoose"
The Cablehouse-Unique steel-frame building all of logging cable that weighs about 26 tons (slightly more than the Burl up the road)
Valley of 1000 Faces-Parklike forest with faces painted on wood slabs

Sointula

Finnish Fishing Village-Walk, relax, enjoy local culture

Sooke

Sooke Region Museum-Historical artifacts, scale models, pictures & video showing Sooke, weavings & carvings by Salish & Nootka Indians, major Fine Arts Show during summer

Telegraph Cove

Picturesque village on pilings-Walk, enjoy
Good salmon fishing
Trips to killer whales near Robson Bight

20

Diving the Sooke Potholes.

Tofino

Clayoquot Days Celebration in July
Meares Island & Fort Defiance
Nature Cruises to observe Gray Whales & Sea Lions
Maquinna Marine Park-Natural Hot Springs accessible only by boat or plane, 30min hike from Government Dock at Hot Springs Cove, 3 pools surrounded by natural rock walls

Ucluelet

Wickaninnish Centre-Pacific Rim National Park, Outstanding undersea and Indian Culture Exhibits

Victoria

Royal Victoria Marathon-Sponsored by Victoria Marathon Society. You can enter the Marathon or 8K Fun Race, as runner or in a wheelchair

Royal Victoria Marathon of 1986 starts in front of Legislature Buildings.(Brian Davis)

Afternoon Teas in Victoria-Many famous locations, including the Blethering Place, B.C. Provincial Museum, & The Empress Hotel

Anne Hathaway's Cottage & The Olde England Inn-Replica of the birthplace of William Shakespeare's wife, Curiosity Shoppe

Art Gallery of Greater Victoria-Permanent & visiting collections

Bastion Square-Original site of Fort Victoria

Beacon Hill Park-Beautiful main city park

British Columbia Provincial Museum & Thunderbird Park Totem Poles -Every traveler should see

Butchart Gardens-Floral showpiece of North America, impressive roses, often crowded

The Carillon-Next to B.C. Provincial Museum, gift from the Netherlands.

Find out schedule from Travel Infocentre. Be at tower base 20 minutes early to climb 85 steps leading to the Carillonneur's playing cabin to witness a recital. Very worthwhile.

Classic Car Museum-Rotating exhibit of classic cars

Craigdarroch Castle-Built by Robert Dunsmuir from Scotland 1880's

Craigflower Manor & School-Historic farmhouse & oldest standing schoolhouse in Western Canada, ca1855

Crystal Garden-Tropical garden with 250 species of plants,

exotic birds, monkeys, fish. Stores & afternoon tea

Dominion Astrophysical Observatory-1.8 m telescope & displays, Saturday evenings only, except winter

Emily Carr Gallery of the Provincial Archives of British Columbia

Pacific Undersea Gardens Ltd-Natural aquarium, over 5000 local specimens, live scuba diver shows

Parliament Buildings-30 minute tour year round, learn about Canada's legislative procedure

Royal London Wax Museum-Ancient wax artistry, 200 famous & infamous

Tally-Ho & Sightseeing Co. Ltd.-1 hour horse drawn tour of Victoria, fully narrated, bring your camera

For boxfuls of brochures or special information, contact Tourism Association of Vancouver Island (Ch 16).

Victoria Harbour cabbies.

Couple bicycle Vancouver Island on Hwy 19 west of Sayward.

2. BICYCLING & DRIVING

Freewheeling the open road spells adventure in any country. On Vancouver Island you will find special rewards more often for less work than any other place you could ride on earth.

Distances are short. The longest continuous paved road, the main highway running the length of the Island between Port Hardy and Victoria, is only 544 km (338 mi). North of Nanaimo, this road is Hwy 19. South of Nanaimo, the road is Canadian Hwy 1 (Ch 19, Maps). The distances between places you will want to stop and see are much shorter, sometimes only a few kilometers. In fact, your biggest chal-lenge in planning a bike trip on Vancouver Island is choosing your itinerary from the many options.

Hills are low with gentle grades. The highest paved pass is only 385 m on Hwy 4 east of Port Alberni past Mt. Arrowsmith. Of course, if you ride logging roads or trails, altitude and steepness can increase sharply. Low alpine elevations give your cardiovascular system an edge--a lot less strenuous than a 3300 m pass in the Colorado Rockies. At this latitude with clear skies you can pedal just a few hundred meters up to snowfields and get knockout views of mountains and harbors, islands and ocean.

Or you might get a great view of your knuckles on the handlebars and nothing but whiteout everywhere else. That's the chance you take in this country. That's why rain gear is as much a part of your bike wear here as your helmet. Actually, the weather here is good. Compared to the mainland Pacific Northwest, Vancouver Island weather is exceptionally temperate, and the east side is relatively dry. The summer season, June through August, has many clear days.

Road conditions vary wildly. So does the traffic. If you are traveling off-season (I like the low-key feeling), allow for flooding or icing. Some roads are wide with smooth shoulders and little traffic. Others are narrow gut-clenchers with no place to go when the odd logging truck hits his Jake brakes just behind your left ear. Leaving Victoria and heading up Hwy 1 at

Bicycling

5 o'clock in Friday evening commute traffic is probably not a wise idea, as my friend Tacy found out on a bicycle trip to Vancouver Island in June. Bicycling books in Ch 18 give you clever routes to avoid Island traffic.

Tacy Weeks is an exercise physiologist doing research and teaching in the San Francisco area. A world traveler, she formerly owned a mountaineering store, later a bicycle shop. Tacy and friend Jed bicycled up the Pacific Coast from Lake Tahoe, California, then waited a week in the Seattle area for a couple, David and Rene, who joined them from Rhode Island. They rode the Princess Marguerite ferry to Vancouver Island.

"Jed and I had all the maps. We had chosen where we wanted to go -- up Hwys 1 & 19 to the top of Vancouver Island. We were on 15 speed touring bikes carrying about 75-80 lbs each, more than we needed. Our panniers were low riders on the front and rear. I packed the tools right under the seat. Tools I knew I wouldn't need were buried in the back at the bottom. Most accessible were my wallet, rain jacket and my journal. Jed kept his camera handy. Food was pretty darned accessible.

"From Campbell River north, with the exception of Sayward, were logging camps (Woss, Nimpkish Lake). It was really hot when we were on the Island. One day the only shade was a 1 m shed shadow at Woss. Water was hard for us to come by up on the north end, and this was early season. When we got water we weren't sure of, we used iodine drops, and nobody got sick.

"We were totally self-sufficient, the best way to go. We shopped in grocery stores 3-4 meals ahead. When we came to bulk food stores or supermarkets, we bought quality cereals for breakfast, and for dinner--whole wheat noodles, ragu sauce fresh vegetables, and grated cheese. A real treat was instant pudding. We'd shake it up in our water bottles.

"I had breathable raingear. We got wet on the Oregon Coast. But you sweat in totally waterproof gear. So our choice was a change of clothes and using the dryers at laundromats. We had only 2 periods of rain on Vancouver Island and they happened at night.

Bicyclist debarks the *Lady Rose* at Ucluelet, B.C.

"For women -- I took a summer dress along that turned out to be cool, nice to wear around camp or out in the evening. Taking bicycling shorts and long pants plus leg warmers works really well. After a cold morning, when you warm up, you can pull off the leg warmers without having to undress. If a woman is doing a bicycle trip on her own [Tacy has bicycled throughout the mountains of western Canada and the U.S. by herself], it's a good idea when you pull into a campground to introduce yourself to the campground hosts. Some-times they'll invite you to camp nearby. I rarely did because I wanted to write in my journal, meditate, cook my dinner. You have to like solitude or you wouldn't be traveling that way in the first place. But often in the evening I would sit around the campfire with them. Hosts would often let me put my food in their trailer to keep it safe from bears.

"The advantage of traveling on Vancouver Island is that you can plan shorter trips -- say, Nanaimo to Campbell River -- and stay in hotels if you want. I feel very comfortable on a bike here. Islanders are so friendly. The bicycle is an automatic card to talk to people."

27

"We got to Victoria in the early afternoon, went to the Museum, shopped, then wanted to get out to camp. We were leaving town during rush hour. That first day, we went only 16 km to Thetis Lake. We had the most traffic between Victoria and Nanaimo that we saw since leaving Lake Tahoe, except for Seattle. Next day we rode 102 km to a campground on a lake in Cedarville close to the airport (I loved watching all of the floatplanes). It was flatter than I expected, only 353 m over Malahat Pass, but continuous views of boats and bays in Finlayson Arm, Squally Reach, and Saanich Inlet.

"We had ferry reservations out of Port Hardy that we had to make way in advance. It was June 13th and the ferry was departing June 19th. With over 480 km to go, we couldn't just goof off. The next night was Courtenay, 124 km, flat to rolling hills with blankets of wildflowers all day long. I was impressed with all the different tribal poles. We wished we knew more about Native art, about the culture of the Island, before going up there.

"Next day, we bucked stiff wind all day, but it made the water completely dark blue. On a rest stop at Oyster Bay, we could see the peaks across the Strait of Georgia on the mainland. The foreground had grey logs sticking out into the water with streaks of dandelions and purple vetch between them, snowcapped peaks behind. That was thrilling. The stretch up to Campbell River was beautiful -- sculpted clouds, little thin cumulous It was staying light until 9 o'clock at night, so we could ride. We had all made pannier rain covers that just slipped over the packs with elastic edges. Rene and David's were red and ours were yellow. I wrote in my log 'feeling like a multi-colored Chinese dragon, snaking through town.' By switching our positions, we could change our colors like a snake shedding his skin. The visibility for drivers was great. We stayed in Elk Falls at Campbell River, 53 km, with a nature trail leading to the river out the back of our camp.

"North for 93 km the next day. We had to hunt for a place to camp 25 km north of Sayward. We kept going because the road was steep on both sides. Once we left Campbell River, we left civilization. We were warned of bears on a hill past Sayward. A bald eagle swooped overhead, his bright white head still showing after he landed in a tree. We have to keep the water bottles full. Camped on an abandoned logging road. Forest had sphagnum moss, vines with white flowers growing everywhere. The bugs were out en masse.

"The next day after we lunched in Port McNeil, ruffed grouse came running out of the bushes clucking and chasing me as far as she could down the highway. Farther along we saw a cub bear on the road. But thinking about his mother, we didn't stop. We rode 89 km and camped in Port Hardy, then caught the ferry up to Prince Rupert. I want to go back."

Many travelers come to Victoria, stay a few days, and never go north, not realizing that some of the Island's best features, the least traveled land, lie north of Campbell River.

Bicyclists Wes Slaymaker & Nick Sprague at Sproat Lake. Rode from New Mexico to Vancouver Island. Carrying rice & oranges. 3709 km so far.

Bicycling

Here are 7 bicycle holiday routes I recommend. You need maps (Ch 19, Maps -- esp. Provincial Parks for camping). Booking hotels (Ch 17, Hotels) or roughing it, and how many kilometers to ride each day are your decisions. How long you play at each destination is also your option. That's part of the adventure. Do not hesitate to contact the Tourism Association of Vancouver Island or local Infocentres (see Ch 16, Tourist Information) for more details, esp. current road conditions. Be sure to check ferry schedules and make reservations well in advance.

1. Port Hardy -- 45 km -- Port McNeill -- Ferry -- Malcolm Island (Sointula -- Finnish fishing village) -- Ferry -- Cormorant Island (Alert Bay -- U'Mista Cultural Centre, hiking, watch killer whales) -- Ferry -- Port McNeill -- 45 km -- Port Hardy.

2. Port Hardy -- 10 km -- Fort Rupert (Northwest Coast Native Art) -- 18 km -- Coal Harbour -- Ferry -- Quatsino (Reservations) -- Ferry -- Coal Harbour 20 km -- Port Hardy.

3. Campbell River -- 45 km -- Strathcona Park (hiking, kayaking, canoeing) -- 45 km -- Gold River (caving) -- 115 km -- Muchalat Inlet: Nootka Sound Services (Boat trip - Uchuck III: Reservations) -- 15 km -- Gold River -- 88 km -- Campbell River.

4. Port Alberni -- 142 km -- Tofino (Hike Meares Island, watch grey whales, boat/fly to Ahousat & Hot Springs Cove) -- 10 km -- Long Beach -- 30 km -- Ucluelet (Boat trip - *Lady Rose*: Reservations, to Port Alberni)

5. Expand Trip 4. by starting in Nanaimo -- 47 km -- Qualicum Beach- 58 km - Port Alberni (to Trip 4. then return to Nanaimo)

6. Victoria -- 61 km -- Duncan -- 27 km -- Lake Cowichan -- 89 km -- Victoria

7. Victoria -- 35 km -- Sooke (Sooke Museum, potholes) -- 25 km -- Point No Point -- 46 km -- Port Renfrew (West Coast Trail) -- 106 km -- Victoria.

Bicycle shops in Victoria and some towns up-Island rent mountain bikes or touring bikes with panniers. If you plan to ride logging roads, you will need a mountain bike with good tires, heavy duty rims, tools, and a good tire repair kit. *Bicycling Vancouver Island and The Gulf Islands* by Simon Priest with maps by Kimberley Klint (Ch 18, Good Reading) is sold at bookstores and bike shops (256 pages, 110 maps) and covers important corridors on the Islands. The *B.C. Bicycling Guide* by Teri Lydiard is reportedly available at some bookstores and bike shops, and has elevation profiles. The Mountaineers of Seattle have published several bicycling books including *Bicycling The Backroads of Northwest Washington & Backroads Around Puget Sound* by Erin and Bill Woods (several tours on B.C. roads covering Victoria and the Fraser Valley).

From sources listed in Ch 19, Maps, you can get Eagle Eye Maps, showing Gulf Islands, Victoria, the Saanich Peninsula and more, that are made to fit standard handlebar bag windows and show all roads with suggested tours, hills, and services.

Note daylight changes: Sunrise times--December 8 am; June 5 am. Sunset times--December 4 pm; June 9 pm

Contact: **Bicycling Association of British Columbia**, 1200 Hornby Street, Vancouver, B.C. V6Z 2E2, (604) 669-BIKE (24-hour information hotline).

Sunshine in Victoria, B.C.

Larry Kuhl and pink salmon (humpy), Campbell River, B.C.

3. FISHING: FRESHWATER TO SALTWATER

Fly Fishing By A Native Angler

by Eric Jamieson

Island streams, rivers and estuaries host all five species of Pacific salmon -- chinook (spring, tyee, king), coho (silver), chum (dog), pink (humpy) and sockeye, plus both resident (freshwater) and anadromous (sea-run) natural and stocked rainbow trout, cutthroat trout, brook trout, brown trout and Dolly Varden char. There are also small pockets of kokanee (landlocked sockeye salmon). You can drive to most points on the Island in a day or less and many of the most popular and pro-ductive streams, rivers and lakes are close to settlements. For the more adventurous angler, boats, helicopters and the old Canadian Beaver will put you onto a pristine river in minutes, where you can fight it out with the bears for your fish.

Fly fishing for any Pacific salmon is usually done in saltwater estuaries, although some hatcheries do allow river angling for coho (please refer to both freshwater and saltwater regulations before angling). The earliest I have ever fly fished for salmon (salmon are commonly caught on fly rods in salt water by trolling large polar bear flies behind swiftly moving boats) is July, and that for the smallest of them -- the pink salmon. Although the pink is considered more a commercial species than a sport fish, and sport fishermen often shun it due to sporting and meat quality, I look forward to my July jaunts to several rivers where the humpies are fresh and will take a fly. They are protected in fresh water. Therefore, you must angle for them in salt-water estuaries or directly in the salt water.

I recall one such morning several years ago. The river I was fishing is not in a populated area, so it usually attracts only those die-hards who are out for sport. Together with a friend from California, we were the first on the river that morning. As we slipped and slid toward the mouth on the greasy popping wrack (seaweed) that covered the tidal flats, we could hear the fat smack of a fish or two striking the river surface. At dawn we could see a school of pinks milling about the mouth, porpoising in their peculiar fashion. Into their midst we cast our #6 hot pink streamer flies, similar to salt water shrimps. Several casts later my fly was taken, the line straightening with an electrifying jolt. Out of the brine rocketed a well-hooked pink. Jumping several times, it did its best to shake the hook (pinks are very adept at this). However, it held and I soon beached a bright 4-pounder.

Later , about October, you can catch coho salmon similarly in rivers where they are legal (see regulations) but more often in saltwater estuaries. Coho are big fish and easily top 10 pounds, although 6 or 7 is more common. Taking a #2 blue and white polar/bucktail fly, not unlike a coronation fly, they will test an angler's skill to the nth degree. Once hooked, they run just under the surface, leaping several times in head shaking frenzies. Although I have never successfully fly fished for coho in salt water (only saltwater estuaries), there are several places on the Island where you can take coho from shore. Usually, they do not move into shallow water until later in the season (August), but when they do you can see them actively feeding and jumping. There, I have heard, they will take a small bait fish pattern. In the river they stop feeding and hug the bottoms of the deep holes, moving mostly at night. To reach them, you need a weighted hook or a couple of feet of lead core line.

Two other species found in estuaries during fall sometimes follow the salmon to their spawning grounds, coastal cutthroat trout (cutts will butt the stomachs of female salmon to get them to spill their eggs) and Dolly Varden char. The cutts are my favorite fish, despite their usual small size. Along several cutty reaches I like, you can see fat yellow-bellies almost all year. One beach in Victoria has been produc-tive right into December. I have fished it successfully with a #8 orange winged muddler even when there has been snow on the beach. But most of my cutt fishing has been fair weather sport, sometimes using a weighted stonefly nymph.

Leaping salmon, Campbell River, B.C.

My experience with Dolly Varden char was unplanned. I was after pink salmon but arrived a week too early. No pinks, but the odd cutt was surfacing in the river mouth. Rather than waste the day I tried the pink streamer flies I had labored to tie the night before. I had no luck with the cutts. In fact I have never caught a cutt in that estuary. Before I knew it, though, I was into one of the best fly fishing days of my life. The fish I caught were beautifully colored, with fine red rosettes patterning their metallic bodies. It took me a while to identify them, for I had never seen an anadromous Dolly before. As fast as I released one, I had another on. Although I have caught many freshwater Dollies, I have never seen that many in fresh water. Freshwater fish also seem to be smaller and paler than their saltwater cousins.

In winter new life stirs in the river -- the jewel of the Island fly fisher, the steelhead trout, actually anadromous rainbow trout. They have been known to exceed 30 pounds. Here on the Island the largest hatchery fish I know of was taken from the Little Qualicum River a couple of winters ago and weighed 23.5 pounds. The difference between these steel grey, snow bellied, snake-like fish and the salmon that precede them is that the steelhead recover after spawning, while the salmon perish in the act. Steelhead are commonly caught on the fly, although in the winter months high water often makes this impossible. The best time to fly fish for steelhead is March/April, when the rivers are lower and the water clear. Granted, you catch a higher percentage of kelts (spawned-out steelhead) at this time, but most of us release our steelhead anyway (see regs regarding the capture of wild/hatchery steelhead).

Once, in March, while fishing in the Campbell River, I cast a #2 general practicioner far upstream several times with no result. I shortened the line to cover new water. Just before the fly began its inward sweep at the end of its run, a fish struck heavily. I set the hook and watched the line peel from my reel as the fish raced downstream. Stumbling after it trying to turn its head, I soon had a bright 12-pound buck finning quietly in the shallows next to my feet. I held him for a minute or two while he recovered, before he suddenly darted away into the current.

Steelhead fishing is not only a winter sport. Several Vancouver Island rivers support summer steelhead, a few over 15 pounds. There is nothing better, on a warm summer morning, than to cast a steelhead bee or a large doc spratley into the sun-dappled shallows of some boulder-strewn Island river. These fish will even take a bright orange general practitioner at this season, although I always associate this fly with winter. One 10-pound summer steelhead, accepting the small trout pattern of a friend of mine, tested the breaking strength of his #5 graphite fly rod several times during a few harrowing attempts to break loose.

Fly fishing opportunities on Vancouver Island are in the 1000's. Despite years of fly fishing for steelhead, cutts, brook trout (Spectacle Lake) and bass (Elk Lake), I doubt I have covered 10% of them. This abundance may overwhelm the visiting angler. Although here it is impossible to cover it all, let me suggest how a traveler, new to the area, might plan a fly fishing holiday.

Wherever you land on the Island, the major towns have sporting goods shops where the owners know the local fly fishing spots. Often sport fishing represents the major commerce of the area.

Contact the local Travel Infocentre, and the Tourism Association of Vancouver Island, who will help make your stay as interesting and enjoyable as possible. They will contact resorts for you, organize freshwater guides, or just provide maps and good old-fashioned directions on how to get to the local trout hole. If an Infocentre is not available, and you are still determined to fish that river or stream that you read about in some magazine or book last winter, pick up one of the many complete angling guides to the province. The first section is

Flyfisherman reviving a pink salmon with back-and-forth movement in swift water, Campbell River, B.C.

usually Region #1: Vancouver Island. In these magazine-like angling guides, you will learn what species are listed for a particular water-course, what season is best, where it is (by map), including other valuable information, such as boat launching facilities. I have found the most comprehensive guide is the *Okay Anglers B.C. Fishing Directory & Atlas*, produced by Bill Hoshizaki of Kelowna. You can get this publication in sporting goods shops around the province or by writing to: Hoshi Enterprises, 753 Kinnear Ave., Kelowna, B.C., Canada V1Y 5B2.

You need durable waders for most streams, rivers and estuaries, with solid wading boots soled with either caulks or felt (a must). Since many rivers are fairly swift, especially in fall/winter high water conditions, I recommend a wading staff. A small boat is essential for lake fishing. Vancouver Island lakes are typically edged with water reeds, making fly casting difficult. If you are a fly fisherman already, you will know what weight rod to bring for a 1- or 2-pound cutt, a 10-pound coho or a 15-pound steelhead. Flies will vary with the game fish. Pick them up locally. You can never beat local knowledge. Bring your own along as well. It is always nice to share a quiet moment on the river with another angler, talk a little shop, exchange a fly or two and wish each other well. Oh, don't forget your camera! How else will you show off your 12-pound summer steelhead to your buddies back home?

What about the future of fly fishing on Vancouver Island? As you must be aware, industry, including logging, mining, and manufacturing, has threatened many ecosystems. Compromise is the new environmental rule. Perhaps compromise is what we, who view the resource for more than its dollar value, must accept if we are to have any say at all. This does not mean that whole ecosystems will be saved for us, although some have. More likely it means sharing the area with multiple resource users. Water. Without it, the future of our fish and our sport looks dismal. But I am optimistic. There is a dawning realization that clean water is as important to local commerce as it is to the fish that thrive in it. Water quality, I hope, will be the winner in this struggle, for without it we will all lose.

Eric Jamieson

Eric has lived in British Columbia most of his life and has written for magazines and newspapers for the past 10 years. The environment is a favorite topic, and he writes both outdoor and history articles. Besides freelance writing, he is also a photographer. Married, with 2 children, Jamieson lives and works on Vancouver Island.

Good news for travelers! Island streams are "flashy" -- during and just after a heavy rain they may muddy up and be very poor fishing, but a couple of days later they may clear up for great fishing. So don't give up.

Bass

There are at least 15 bass lakes on the south coast of British Columbia. Blackburn Lake and Saint Mary's Lake on Saltspring Island have smallmouth bass. Bass in Prospect Lake near Victoria will often go 4 lbs. Other Vancouver Island bass hotspots are: Florence, Glen, Young, Langford, Matheson Elk, and Shawnigan Lakes. Five notable lakes between Nanaimo and Qualicum -- Holden, Long, Divers, Spider and Quennell -- all have smallmouth. Springtime is the best bass fishing, but it carries throughout the summer season until September. This non-native fish provides good sport for Island travelers.

The Lakes of Vancouver Island is a Fishing Guide published and available through the Ministry of Environment and Parks, Recreational Fisheries Branch (address below). British Columbia has thousands of lakes with high quality fishing for Rainbow and Brown trout, Cutthroat, Steelhead, Smallmouth bass, Dolly Varden, and Kokanee. The Island has hundreds of lakes with outstanding fishing. Many of them appear in this Guide: -locations and access routes;
-dates and types of the best fishing on each lake;
-launching and accommodation/camping information;
-stocking records that are updated periodically by an

appendix;

-maps of the general area (advise obtaining detailed topographic and logging road maps from sources in Ch 19. Maps, the Forestry Service, logging companies, or retail stores). Note in Ch. 9, Habitat, several local expert references to fishing lakes and streams.

While you have to hike to some backcountry lakes, many are accessible by vehicle. Remember, though, meeting a fast-moving logging truck unexpectedly, or leaving your car parked on the road, especially at curves, can shorten the life of you or your car. Use caution. Yield to trucks. Pay attention to posted signs describing active logging and closures. The TFL (tree farm license) of major logging companies gives them jurisdiction over much area use, so the Guide notes "camping by permission" for lakes in forest company property. When you plan to camp in these places, notify logging companies at their offices in case of blasting or treefalling operations that may deny access. When you are in an area without formal camping or picnic facilities, **do not build an open fire** !

(Yearly) **British Columbia Non-Tidal Water Sport Fishing Regulations** are available in most sporting goods retail shops. For **licenses and information**, travelers who live outside the Province, contact: Recreational Fisheries Branch, Ministry of Environment and Parks, Parliament Buildings, Victoria, B.C. V8V 1X5. For specific, **local fishing information** on Vancouver Island, contact the Fisheries Branch staff at Regional Headquarters: Recreational Fisheries Branch, Ministry of Environment and Parks, 2569 Kenworth Road, Nanaimo, B.C. V9T 4P7 (604) 758-3951.

Salmon

Campbell River, B.C. has long called itself the "Salmon Capital of the World." Now, Port Alberni advertises itself as the "Salmon Capital of the World." All you have to do is look at the size of the commercial fishing fleet in the harbor at Port Hardy and you know instantly where there's another "Salmon Capital of the World". The truth is that the entire west coast of British Columbia, particularly the water surrounding

Alan Pineo and his 43 lb chinook (spring, tyee, king), Tofino, B.C.

Vancouver Island, is the **real** salmon capital. Fishing derbies from the north end of the Island to Victoria prove that there are still many elusive tyee -- over 60 lbs -- in these waters. In fact, recent catch reports and habitat analyses indicate that the salmon are recovering in both numbers and size (Ch 9. Habitat).

Hundreds of individual charter boats operate on both coasts. Dozens of local guide brochures are available at every Travel Infocentre on the Island. Associations you may contact include: Nanaimo Fishing Guide Association, 777A Poplar Street, Nanaimo, B.C. V9S 2H7, (604) 754-6744 and Port Hardy Charter-Boat Association, Box 95, Port Hardy, B.C. V0N 2P0, (604) 949-2628. Many fly-in, boat-in or drive-in fishing lodges offer a wide variety of charter services, both daily fishing adventures and package vacations. Contact: Tourism Association of Vancouver Island (Ch 16).

Discovery Pier -- Canada's first saltwater fishing pier -- is a great Island attraction. Now, without a boat, even from a wheelchair, you can fish the clear Campbell River Harbor waters for salmon and other saltwater fish. The pier has beautiful design: nearly 200 m long, benches and fishing seats, built-in rod holders, built-in bait stations, night lighting and weather shelters, fish cleaning stations, scales, restrooms, phones, even a place to eat clam chowder and chicken or beef souvlaki in pita bread besides the usual hot dogs, potato chips, chocolate bars, and hot and cold drinks. Definitely a family place, the pier is close to downtown stores, public transit buses stop nearby, and there is a large parking lot for cars, buses and bicycles. It's intended for year-round use, and you can catch good-sized salmon from the pier along with lots of local bottom fish because of the extensive artificial reef created just below the pier.

Discovery Pier in Campbell River, B.C., has riprap designed to enhance marine habitat, so you can fish for the big ones without a boat.

Each summer and fall on Vancouver Island, you and your family can see salmon spawning in rivers you can drive to. While these are the peak periods, spawning starts before these dates and continues later (for more exact, yearly data, contact the Department of Fisheries and Oceans below):

Date	River	Area	Species
10-30 Sept	Quinsam Hatchery	Campbell River	Chinook
20-30 Nov	Cowichan	Duncan	Coho
20 Nov-10 Dec	Cowichan	Duncan	Chums
Oct	Big Qualicum	Qualicum Beach	Coho
20 Nov-10 Dec	Big Qualicum	Qualicum Beach	Chums
1-10 Nov.	Goldstream	Victoria (Malahat)	Spring
1-10 Nov	Goldstream	Victoria (Malahat)	Coho, chums

Many fishing guide services will freeze, can, or otherwise process your catch for you and send it to your destination.

(Yearly) **British Columbia Tidal Water Sport Fishing Guide** and the **Regulations** are available in most sporting goods shops. For licenses and information, travelers who live outside the Province, contact: Department of Fisheries & Oceans, Communications Branch, 1090 West Pender Street, Vancouver, B.C. V6E 2P (604)666-2268, 24-hour service, (604)388-3252 (in Victoria). **Red Tide updates available.**

Trolling near Broken Islands Group, Barkley Sound, B.C.

Totem at Long Beach, Pacific Rim National Park.

4. ENJOYING ART

Mackjack Fever

by
Julia Moe

The trip down the mackjack
was bound to be
a journey of importance.
we started the trail
at five in the afternoon,
already in full sweat
from a long and dusty search
for its beginning.
we knew
it was a two-hour hike
through uncut river swamp,
poorly marked at best.
from there two hours
down the winding tidal mouth
of the river,
not knowing
if the three of us
would fit in the canoe
(if we found it),
or if the tide
would be with us or against us.
the trip down the mackjack
grabbed us like a sudden fever
that broke apart our lives,
bodies struggling over
windfall after windfall,
stumbling and scraping
our way through thickets

of salmonberry,
a patch of devil's club
like a nightmare vision.
i did not even know
it grew in this country.
we found the canoe
and fit all of us
in and out several times
working our way over logjams
and paddling harder
as the tide flowed in
against us,
the day darkening
and the river widening
but winding on,
bending yet again
around one more corner,
all three of us
paddling by the time
we saw the cabin
at the neck of the river,
surf breaking white on the moon-soft beach
of the opposite shore.
the trip down the mackjack
was like folding back
the slick cover of a magazine
and finding ourselves
flat on a photograph
that quickened to depth.
our bodies rolled off
the edge of the page,
hollowed out the hot white sand,
plunged holes through breakers.
salt and sweat and water and sun
washed over us,
shimmered mirages

off the ocean,
delirious visions
at the height of summer fever.
that trip down the mackjack
left us leaning
against the side of the truck,
thirsty for beer,
ready for steaks,
thorn-scratched and fly-bitten,
sun-burned and sand-raw,
shins bruised,
all battered and used up
like invalids past the breaking
of the mackjack fever.

The Mackjack River gathers water from the west side of Mt. Brandes above the northwest coast of Vancouver Island and carries it down into Raft Cove. Into the sea. Julia Moe, Cape Scott dweller and former lighthouse keeper, lives with her husband Ron in Holberg.

Clarence Mills

Haida Name: Gah-ghin-skuss (Out of your own land)

Family Crests: Split Raven, Grizzly Bear

The artist, whose work appears on the back cover and title page of this book, was born into the Wilson family at Skidegate, Queen Charlotte Islands. His Na-nai (grandmother: Kathleen Hans) told his mother that he was destined to be a Haida carver -- a reincarnation of her late husband Isaac Hans, a renowned Heida artist. His great grand-father Henry Young, also a great Haida carver, gave Clarence his Haida name.

Inspired by the culture of his ancestors, Clarence began over a decade ago studying totems of argillite and cedar. To capture the traditional spirit and strength of his culture while developing his own intricate, integrated style, he sought the simple, smooth flow of the Haida art. For 5 years he taught himself the demanding art.

Clarence Mills, artist, with his first totem.

Clarence now lives and works on Vancouver Island. His work is available in limited edition prints, carvings in argillite, ivory, cedar and, more recently, in silver and gold. After carving a 10-foot red cedar totem in the Folklife Pavillion at the Vancouver Expo, he has been commissioned to carve totems for international as well as Canadian projects.

The man is bold and brave as his art. What about the future of Northwest Coast Native Art? --"It will continue to enhance the beauty of the culture. The culture will survive through the art."--Clarence Mills.

"Whaling Wall XIII" by Wyland.

See the mural painted on the side of Chandler's Restaurant in Victoria--killer whales of local A-5 pod painted life size in 12 days, each mammal showing the markings of an actual whale identified in the wild--done in memory of underwater filmmaker Robin Morton. Characterized as one of the capital's most gentle citizens-of-the-world, Morton was a student and chronicler of the killer whale. He helped turn Robson Bight into an ecological reserve. He was studying the A-5 pod when he drowned at Robson Bight in 1986, just days before a National Geographic television crew was to start filming a documentary on his life and work.

Land of 1000 Faces by Hetty Fredrickson

Graduate of the Academy of Creative Art in Holland, Hetty came to Canada in 1963, with 2 little boys. She found survival tough in the North American West and settled down on Vancouver Island to marry a logger. She points to a painted driftwood log of totem character with an eye at ground level: "When we are born, we 'know it all' (lifting her finger up the piece of wood), then we are confronted as children growing up with all the confusions of life, then the mask comes off and we are idealistic (finger moves higher still), then we mature into being more realistic (then at the top, where there is no paint but only a knob of wood that could be a smiling beaver snout), finally we become the basic animal we are!" She laughs.

In her park gallery near Sayward, it's cool and green under the forest canopy with some clearing of the natural understory. The path winds around, curving past rocks and ferns. I see a forbidding face painted on a stump guarding a door set into the stump. The door has a knob. Instinctively, I reach out and grasp the knob. Of course the door does not open because it is only an illusion. The journey continues with hundreds of faces jumping into my view as I look left and right. Painted rounds of native wood leaning against trees and rocks, nailed up on trees at eye level or higher. Faces laughing, smirking, winking, gaping, pensive. When I get to the White River and a

Hetty Fredrickson in her Sayward gallery. Caption below painting with embedded pennies: "They searched and searched for happiness
Depicted by a cent.
They never saw their coins inside
And on and on they went."

couple of benches, I am ready to sit down and stare into the faceless water. Then on to Indian masks, faces grimacing out of an old car frame, bug-eyes, closed eyes, Groucho Marx. They're all here -- TV friends, political enemies. Toward the end they cascade at me in a jarring jumbling finale. I think she intended them that way -- bizarre, magnificent. At the exit, at a simple unadorned hunk of pure jade, Hetty has the last laugh.

"The Little Town That Did"--Chemainus

"'The Little Town That Did,' a documentary film of the past, present, and future of an unusual West Coast former milltown, Chemainus, B.C., had its world premier on Vancouver Island in the spring of 1984. It's the story of how, on the brink of becoming a ghost town, Chemainus commissioned well known artists to literally "paint the town" with gigantic exterior murals showing the area's early history. It is the story of the renaissance of a milltown.

"The film deals with colour and music and entertainment...murals seem to paint themselves in scenes of time-lapse magic. The deserted hulk of the once powerful sawmill reverberates once again with the call of its fondly remembered steam whistle. The story is told, not by a 'hired voice' narrator, but through actual comments by the mural artists and town residents. The music is an unusual combination of traditional string and wind instruments, blended with modern electronic synthesizers.

"It is also the story of a small, depressed, one-industry town, not unlike hundreds of other one-industry towns, that rejects the death sentence imposed upon it by changing economics."-in video or 16mm from "Chemainus Film Productions" Box 488, Chemainus, B.C. V0R 1K0

Chemainus mural.

"End of the Trail" (White winged scoters). Timothy Hume, artist.

Art and history are inseparable: artists make history. Many of the galleries and art centers on Vancouver Island are part of museums. The U'mista Cultural Centre in Alert Bay is one. There are "don't miss this" galleries that give you quickly a lasting understanding of particular Island styles. Tony Hunt's Arts of the Raven Gallery in Victoria is that way. So is the Emily Carr Gallery in Victoria. There are too many to name here.

After this brief introduction, I hope you are excited by the potential for enjoying Island art -- both Native and white, traditional and contemporary. To find out more, contact the Travel Infocentres or the Tourism Association of Vancouver Island (Ch 16)

Native Dancers.--by Laurie Best, courtesy North Island Gazette.

Chemainus mural.

5. EXPLORING HISTORY

Some facts: After about 8000 years of Indian civilizations on the Island, Spanish explorer Juan Perez sighted Estevan Point in 1774. British explorer James Cook discovered Vancouver Island in 1778, sailing *HMS Discovery* and *HMS Resolution* into Nootka Sound and meeting the Indians. In 1792, George Vancouver, the British explorer for whom the Island is named, surveyed it and later published his findings. Capt. Vancouver met Don Juan Francisco de la Bodega y Quadra at Friendly Cove on the rocky headland where the Spanish built their fort, resulting in Spain abandoning all claims to the Pacific Northwest. In 1849, Vancouver Island became a British crown colony. Since 1866 it has been governed as part of British Columbia.

If you want blood and fire to make these facts come alive, visit Vancouver Island. Residents are so aware of their heritage that part of their business is making their own fascinating history come true for travelers. Come here, meet them, and get them talking about what happened years ago. Many contribute through their **art** or by putting on the clothes, gathering the gear and **doing** what happened--dancing Indian ceremonies, paddling ancient-design sea canoes, firing the noon gun at Nanaimo.

Morning sunshine warms the spaces between the trees and Sooke Museum on the south end of Vancouver Island. Grass beside the building steams off its night dew. A barbeque fire starting in the salmon pit curls smoke into your face. A group of children 7 to 9 years old are waiting to do the tour of Moss Cottage. Elida Peers, whose face smiles all over and reflects the gold light bouncing off her hair into other people's faces, talks to the children like adults, thereby getting their attention.

"Just imagine a long time ago--1902--when there were no cars, no airplanes, no TV, not even the nylon that your jacket is made of. People didn't have many possessions." As Joan Baez

55

would sing, I wonder if you can. "Way back in the old days when people had to really struggle with the dirt road, get out and milk the cow in the morning. Way back before your grandmother was born, this house stood in the woods in Sooke. In the house lived a lady called Matilda Gordon. Let's go see if she's home. You can visit her."

The kids flock over to the rickety front porch. It's a 2-story, smallish structure with dark windows you can't see into. A little bit mysterious. The gutsiest boy knocks on the front door. Footsteps. The door creaks open inward, and a woman wearing a black and white eyelet period dress greets us, waving us inside.

"You are welcome to come in. I must tell you, though, I ran out of oil for one of my lamps, and the living room is a bit dim." Entering is magical.

"No electricity!" one of the boys stage-whispers.

So begins a fine tale that leads from room to room in the old wood house. Real fire in the fireplaces. Real water in the washbasin. Horsehair mattresses. Bamboo fishing poles. Real food cooking in the kitchen. Tiny rooms, actually, that if you're 6 feet tall make you stoop under the doorjams and wonder if, cooped up in this house in the winter with 5 children, no plumbing, and a whole lot of rain coming down, maybe you wouldn't just go crazy. This thought gives you fresh, intense respect for the Canadian pioneers who forged Sooke from the forest and sea.

In 1977, when Sooke Museum opened, 3500 people came. In 1986, 29,000 came. In 1987, in early August, the total visitor count was already over 150,000. A direct tax appropriation passed by the regional district in May 1987, which supports the museum was a great victory and tells you a lot about the strength of community support. Sooke volunteers do all the work. Born and raised in Sooke, Elida is a volunteer par excellence. She left a managerial position in Victoria to run the museum and the art show for free.

Sooke smithy.

Elida talks about Sooke: "Victoria was settled in 1843 when the Hudson's Bay Fur Company Trading Post moved out from Oregon at the mouth of the Columbia for political and boundary reasons. In 1849, the British told the Hudson's Bay Company that they must make land available for settlement in return for control of the land. Captain Walter Colquhoun Grant made the first purchase. He had retired in Scotland. He came out here with a group of 8 labourers, and they established at Sooke, putting in small farms and operating a fort. However, there were only peaceful relations with the native people.

"John Muir also came with his family in 1849, brought out by the Hudson's Bay Company to oversee the mining of coal at Ft. Rupert on the northeast coast of Vancouver Island. The coal industry did not thrive. Muir bought out Grant's land in 1854, establishing the lumbering industry for the province at Sooke. From their first arrival, they were shipping out spars for sailing vessels, pilings for the wharves in San Francisco, and they had a steam sawmill operating by 1855. They used the boilers from the wrecked vessel *Enterprise*, which foundered off Victoria, converting them into their water powered mill. The Muirs and their 4 sons, one became sheriff of Victoria, were the real enterprising builders of the community. Their steam sawmill operated until 1892.

"Moss Cottage was built from lumber cut in that Muir sawmill. It was built for James Welsh, who worked for the Muirs in the sawmill and had 2 sisters married to Muir brothers. In 1869, his bride, Mary Ellen Flynn sailed out here around perilous Cape Horn into Victoria, where she embarked in an Indian cargo canoe up to Woodside, carrying her muslin bridal gown with her... Descendants of that original family are prominant in Sooke today."

A real lighthouse light blinks on the corner of the museum property, its lens capable of focusing with enough intensity to start fires. An immense air tank behind the blacksmith's shop powers the foghorn.

Talking about giant fish traps that used to operate at the mouth of spawning streams on the west coast: "They extended out a half mile, and the pilings were 150 ft. high with a net arrangement that stopped the fish as they were coming in to spawn [and caught just about everything else indiscriminately]. There were lifts [takes] when they had probably 10,000 fish. These were no longer operating after 1958. One of the men who worked there had a 16 mm camera and got very good footage. He allowed us to use it, and we made it into a movie that's running daily all summer now at the Newcombe Theatre, the B.C. Provincial Museum's auditorium, in Victoria. Films run continuously all day on the second floor of the museum. People are free to wander in and out of the upstairs video room. We also have a program for local artists throughout the year. Each artist has a month. We're booked 3 years ahead. We will have the art show again next summer."

At the north end of Vancouver Island, near Cape Scott Park , I am out in the forest with poet Julia Moe and her husband Ron. They used to own property inside Cape Scott, before it became a provincial park. They also spent years keeping lighthouses. As I get to know them a little, I am struck by the parallel between what they have gone through in their lives on Vancouver Island and what the early Danes went through at Cape Scott. They both fought the land...and the land won.

We are walking around on historic property near Holberg where the Moes are the stewards. The former owner was an eccentric named Bernt Ronning. A creek running along the trail from San Josef River to Raft Cove is named after this oldtimer. He cleared and planted about 5 acres of exotic trees and shrubbery, built a cabin, then died. The rainforest is reclaiming the land, so in spare time from his fish farming and her writing, Ron and Julia are clearing the alders and salmonberries out to free up rhododendron bushes (that bloom brilliant yellow and pink and orange flowers), maples, horse chestnuts, male and female monkey trees from Chile and Argentina, bamboo, and walnut. Ron leads us to the rotting old house:

"This place is between the old Cape Scott wagon road and a trail that goes down toward Raft Cove. There were settlers who tried to establish themselves all along that trail. This became an unofficial hotel and center. Ronning had an open house, basically. Hike in and you just stayed overnight. It was the post office and polling booth at different times. The interior of the house is one large room. Some of it is milled lumber, but much is split cedar. He took balsam fir and handsawed it into planks, laid it all down and took giant planes that they braced against their shoulders, and planed this floor. No disk sanders in those days! Waxed it and oiled it. They had a pump organ up there. They would come from Cape Scott, from Holberg, bring boats around from Quatsino on the inlet to Holberg and hike up here. The locals always thought Ronning was nuts. He went to all that trouble to clear out those big trees, and I mean it was a **lot** of trouble, and all he did was plant more trees."

Sitting on top of a high, logged hill looking far down the coastline: "We wanted to see Raft Cove included in the Park. I don't think we're going to win that one, though. They are logging it. It is virgin timber."

The couple recalls how in the "do it your own way 60's" they used to sit at their jobs and wish for life in the backcountry. Finally they got enough money together, bought a 40 acre parcel, cheap, in the backlands of Cape Scott, and built a log cabin. They had to boat materials into a lagoon then hand-haul everything up 2 km of trail they'd built:

"We weren't into chain saws. We were trying to do it with a hand saw. Finally we bought one when we found out we'd be old people before we got the cabin done. Gas for it was a problem, though."

"Few people hiked out to Cape Scott in those days. There was no real trail, and it was so far. If you could even hear a plane, you'd be offended. Swimming with the trees and the animals, it was just what we'd dreamed of. It turned out to be a lot more than we'd bargained for! But we loved it.

"Then a guy at the light had a heart attack. We were available right now, 2 warm bodies. It evolved into our doing relief duty for light-house keepers. We were only supposed to be on lighthouse duty 2 weeks, but it was spring before they got it all sorted out. By then we had decided, let's keep doing it. It's winter. It's pouring down rain. No firewood to cut, a job we enjoy with all the reading, and we're making money. For 12 years, we spent 4-6 months a year and every Christmas on the lighthouse. You buy a pair of boots a year, some dry jeans...you don't have a lot of expenses. We enjoyed it.

"I remember the first time they airlifted equipment to the light with a helicopter. It was a big sky crane, and it took us in to our cabin on the way. We were packing a stove and other heavy stuff we didn't want to drag in up the trail. When we got over the part of the forest where our cabin was, we saw our circle of stone marks, and I signaled the pilot to land. He refused. We begged him to put us down, we'd be all right, we had a warm cabin down there. He just couldn't believe that we actually **lived** out there and didn't want to let us off in the middle of nowhere. Years later, after we became good friends, the pilot still talked about this crazy young couple.

"We never did see the cougar. He saw us. One time Julia went out in new snow to get the axe from a hunter's cabin about a mile away. As she returned she could see that cougar tracks were covering her own. She made record time getting back home!

"I remember the first time we heard the wolves howling. It was a full moonlit night. We didn't have any door on the cabin, just a blanket. There was this eery sound of their howling. We tucked the blanket around the door a little tighter.

"We had trumpeter swans and lots of other waterfowl in the saltwater marshes. The first time I heard trumpeter swans, I'd gone in to do the mail run while Julia stayed back to keep the home fires burning. I was coming back when I heard this trumpeting sound. I thought, hmmm, Julia's having a good time for herself. I wonder what she's up to. As I got closer to the cabin, I saw her behind a tree, fingers up to her lips. We sneaked out into the marshes to take a look. There were the trumpeter swans.

"When the Park went in, we debated about setting up a wilderness resource center. But it would have been a real struggle. So we decided to leave and just be glad for what we've had."

Vancouver Island Musems

For a complete list, contact: **British Columbia Museums Association**, 514 Government St., Victoria, B.C. V8V 4X4 (604) 386-6117. **Call ahead or ask locally** for times and days they are open. Some you will enjoy:

Alert Bay Library and Museum, 199 First Street, Alert Bay, (604) 974-5721: Features Kwakiutl and local history artifacts. Also has a photo and archival collection. St. George's Anglican Chapel built in 1925, is opened for visitors on request.

U'Mista Cultural Centre, Front Street, Alert Bay, (604)974-5403: The museum, housed in a modern cedar building like a Kwakiutl big house, exhibits part of a Potlatch Collection. Visitors are invited to enter the exhibit from the right, as a dancer does at potlatch ceremonies. Viewing the priceless coppers and masks, you learn the story of natives under the potlatch law in letters and reports that are part of the exhibit. "When one's heart is glad, he gives away gifts. It was given to us by our Creator, to be our way of doing things, to be our way of rejoicing, we who are Indian. The potlatch was given to us to be our way of expressing joy." Agnes Alfred, Alert Bay, 1980. The center also displays other historic and contemporary Kwakiutl art and cultural material.

Campbell River & District Museum and Archives, 1235 Island Highway (Tyee Plaza), Campbell River (604) 287-3103: Museum exhibits show Vancouver Island Native cultures, European exploration and pioneer history. The shop is well stocked with contemporary Native art. Guided land and sea field trips enable tourists to visit historic sites.

British Columbia Forest Museum, Hwy 1, Duncan (604) 748-9389: 40 hectares devoted to the history of British Columbia's forests. It has an operating steam railway, films, guided tours, hands-on activities as well as spacious picnic facilities.

Parliament buildings and Victoria Harbour.

Cowichan Valley Museum, 200 Craig Street, Duncan (604) 748-1143: Domestic artifacts, tools and medical equipment displayed in period room settings. Photo and archival collection.

Kaatza Station Museum, 125 South Shore Road, Lake Cowichan (604)749-6142: Located in a former E & N Railway Station, this museum features early farming, railway and logging artifacts and tells of pioneer life in the area. A new attraction for children is a ride on a railway pump car.

The Bastion, Corner of Bastion & Front, Nanaimo (604) 754-4251: Housed in part of the original Hudson's Bay Fort, the Bastion's collection focuses on the period 1850-1880 and includes insignia, hand guns and photographs. Archive of military documents. Features a daily noon cannon salute by Army Cadets.

Craigdarroch Castle, 1050 Joan Crescent off Fort St., Victoria (604) 592-5323: Robert Dunsmuir commissioned the firm of Williams and Smith of Portland, Oregon, to design this impressive landmark in 1890. Many of its 39 rooms are being restored and furnished with period pieces.

Craigflower Heritage Site, 110 Island Hwy, Victoria (604) 387-3067: Site Farm house occupied in 1856, was the home of Kenneth McKenzie, Bailiff of Craigflower Farm, operated by a subsidiary of the Hudson's Bay Company. It has been restored and furnished with some original artifacts. An 1855 Colonial

School House is open on a limited basis and may be booked by school groups during winter months.

Emily Carr Gallery of The Provincial Archives, 1107 Wharf St., Victoria (604) 387-3080: Paintings by the well-known Canadian artist, Emily Carr, and her contemporaries are exhibited here. Shows change regularly.

Fort Rodd Hill National Historic Park and Fisgard Lighthouse National Historic Site, 604 Fort Rodd Hill Road, Colwood (604) 380-4662: Fort Rodd Hill was a site of west coast defenses and has 1890's gun batteries largely intact. Fisgard Lighthouse has been restored to its 1873 appearance. Picnic site.

Maritime Museum of British Columbia, 28 Bastion Sq.,Victoria (604)385-4222: An outstanding collection of artifacts, pictures and ship models tell the story of the sea's influence on the history of British Columbia. Two historic vessels, *Tilikum* and *Trekka*, are on display.

Alberni Valley Museum, Echo Recreation Centre, 4255 Wallace Street, Port Alberni (604) 723-2181: Art and technology are uniquely combined at this museum. Featured are: an operating waterwheel electrical generator, a visitor-operated steam engine and other working displays. Visible storage allows access to a major collection of western Vancouver Island artifacts.

Port Hardy Museum and Archives, 7110 Market Street, Port Hardy (604)949-8143: Go to the Port Hardy Museum to learn about the early white settlers on northern Vancouver Island. Ask about Cape Scott and Sointula on Malcolm Island. Inquire about their popular weekly public programs held during the summer on topics as diverse as Robson Bight whales and hiking on the north Island.

Kwakiutl Museum, Cape Mudge Village, Quathiaski Cove (604) 285-3733: The museum building, inspired by the shape of a sea snail, houses part of a Potlatch Collection. Kwakiutl artifacts such as totem poles and ceremonial regalia. See the petroglyphs near the museum.

Link and Pin Museum, Hwy 19 road to Sayward (604) 282-3678: Features a fine collection of antique kerosene lamps and antique logging equipment, including a large steam donkey. Operated by Fran and Glen Duncan. Next door is "Snoose," a huge wooden logger carved with a chain saw out of a cedar log by artist Henry Stadlbauer. Near the museum is a unique steel-frame building made entirely of used logging cable. The walls contain 2485 m of wire rope and weigh almost 26 tons. Built by Glen Duncan, it opened as a restaurant in 1970. If Glen escorts you through the museum, you will have an unforgetable adventure into the history of Island logging.

Sooke Region Museum, West on Hwy 14, 32 km from Victoria, just west of Sooke River Bridge: The collection includes logging and fishing artifacts, Coast Salish objects and a reconstruction of the Sheringham Lighthouse. Moss Cottage built in 1870, Vancouver Island's only remaining "Tidewater House," is open for tours. Afternoon tea avail-able summer weekends.

British Columbia Provincial Museum, Corner of Belleville and Government Streets, Victoria (604) 387-3701/387-3041: One of the finest museums in British Columbia, the Provincial Museum is known for the high calibre of its exhibits complete with sound effects. Floors of displays cover many aspects of natural and human history. The reconstructed 1900 street scene and the Northwest Coast Native Peoples exhibit are particularly impressive. Thunderbird Park, adjacent to the museum, contains totem poles, a long house and several historic buildings.

Lotaas, "wave-eater," 15 m long Haida war canoe built by Native artist Bill Reid makes 968 km epic voyage from False Creek in Vancouver to Skidegate in the Queen Charlotte Islands, stopping in Prince Rupert and on Vancouver Island for traditional ceremonies. (Laurie Best)

Name	Location	# Holes	Yards	Rating	All Year	Rentals (Carts)	Club House	Dining	Phone
Campbell River Golf & C. C.	Campbell R.	9	6876	69	x	x	x	x	286-4970
Pacific Playground G. C.	"	9	2301		x	x			337-5600
Mount Brenton Golf Club	Chemainus	9	6066	72/69	x	x	x	x	246-9322
Comox Golf Club*	Comox	9	2791	70/65	x	x	x	x	339-4444
Longlands Par 3 G. C.	"	9	1050		Mar/Oct	clubs		x	339-6363
Sunnydale Golf Society	Courtenay	18	5920	72/68	x	x	x	x	334-3342
Galiano Golf & C. C.	Galiano Is.	9	3988	64	x	x	x		539-5533
Pender Is. Golf & C. C.	N. Pender Is.	9	2330	62	x		x	x	629-6659
Saltspring Is. Golf & C. C.**	Saltspring	9	3100	69	x	x	x		537-2121
March Meadows Golf & C.C.	Lk.Cowichan	9	2993	68.5	x	x	x	x	749-6241
Cowichan Golf & C.C.	Duncan	18	6200	70	x	x	x	x	746-5333
Fiddler's Green Golf Ctr.	Nanaimo	9	2100	Par 3	x	x			754-1325
Nanaimo Golf & C.C.*	Nanaimo	18	6554	71.5	x	x	x	x	758-5221
Rutherford Acreage Golf Centre	"	12	1500		x	x	x	x	758-6811
Alberni Golf Club Ltd.	Port Alberni	9	6086	68	x	x	x		723-5422
Pleasant Valley Golf C.	"	9	1200	Par 3	x	x	x		724-5333
Long Beach Golf Course	"	9	3149	71.5	x	x	x		726-7445
7 Hills Golf Course	Port Hardy	9	6060	69.5	x				949-4901
Bring your own clubhouse to this course, which has camper spot, water, electricity.									
Port Alice Golf & C.C.**	Port Alice	9	3860	59.5	x	clubs	x		284-3213
Eaglecrest Golf Club	Qualicum Bch	9	3135	72/70	x	x	x	x	752-6311
Qualicum Beach Memorial Golf Club	"	9	2778	67/66	x	x	x		752-6312
Broome Hill Golf & C.C.	Sooke	9	2295	65/62	x	x	x		642-6344
Ardmore Golf & Fitness Club	N. Saanich	9	2838	66	x	x	x	x	656-4621
Cedar Hill Mun.Golf Cl.	Victoria	18	5100	64	x	x	x	x	595-2823
(Has dress code. Call for reservations.)									
Glen Meadows Golf & C.C.*	N. Saanich	18	6800	73/71	x	x	x	x	656-313
(Visitors welcome. Dress code)									
Gorge Vale Golf Club*	Victoria	18	6382	71	x	x	x	x	383-6451
Henderson Park Golf Course	"	9		Par 3	Mar/Oct	clubs only			595-7946
Metchosin Golf & C.C.	"	9	5354	65	x	x	x	x	478-3266
Mt. Douglas Golf Course	"	9		30	x	x	x		477-8314
Prospect Lk. Golf Course	"	9	2186	63/60	x	x	x	x	479-2688
(Rent clubs and handcarts only. Jr.& Sr. rates.)									
Royal Colwood Golf & C.C.*	"	18	6020/6531	70	x	x	x		478-8331
Royal Oak Golf	"	9	4530	Par 66	x	x			658-1433
(Adj. to Royal Oak Inn. Par is for 18 holes.)									
Uplands Golf Course*	"	18	6246	69.5	x	x	x	x	592-7313
Victoria Golf Club**	"	18	6100	69	x	x	x	x	598-4321
(Guests must be introduced by a member or be member of another club.)									

* Semi-private   ** Private

Warm day with a slight breeze -- perfect for golfing.

6. GOLFING

Year-round golfing is open to you on Vancouver Island--as a des-tination sport, or as an interesting option for days when the water's choppy, to change pace from skiing, or to combine with shopping in town. Many of these links have to be rated the world's most beautiful and highest quality, both for the condition of the fairways and for the views. You can select challenging or easy terrain.

Call ahead to the clubs. Be sure to check with the Tourist Association of Vancouver Island or the nearest Infocentre (both listed in Chapter 16: Tourist Information) because **fees change and new golf centres are opening** all over the Island. Serious golfers who come to the Island specifically to enjoy this sport will want to reserve accommodations in advance in any of the many lodges and hotels from Port Hardy to Victoria.

Mt. Myra (1808 m), Strathcona Park.

7. HIKING & CLIMBING

Walking endless beaches, exploring tidepools, finding Indian petroglyphs, hiking rainforest trails, camping at snowy alpine lakes amid riots of meadow wildflowers, hiking mountain ridges, climbing ice and rock walls--on one Pacific Island? Spread out your map of Vancouver Island and see the basic topography, a northwest to southeast-running backbone of mountains reaching above 2000 m in the middle and tapering off at both ends. Granite crowns the Island. Peaks shouldering permanent snowfields and scattered glaciers, notably the Comox and Cliffe Glaciers, tower over alpine valleys and lakes.

This range is flanked on the west by dense, storm-fed forests and on the east by more open forest linking alpine and subalpine plateaus. Patches of clearcuts or second growth forest occur throughout except in designated wilderness areas or places where companies plan to establish tree farms. The rocky west coast is more rugged, sometimes accessible only by water, but rewards the hiker or climber with privacy and intense beauty. The east coast has wide beaches with more people, drier weather and generally better road access. Exceptions to both are Long Beach on the west coast in Pacific Rim National Park and little known north coast bights and bays.

If you want to do walks and day hikes around towns and casual country areas, every Travel Infocentre (Ch.16) on the Island has local maps and descriptions of guided and self-guiding tours for winter and summer.

Highly recommended for extended camping trips as well as day hikes into southern Island regions are: *Hiking Trails I: Victoria & Vicinity* published by the Outdoor Club of Victoria, Trails Information Society; *Victoria in a Knapsack* by the Sierra Club of Western Canada; *The Naturalist's Guide to the Victoria Region* by Jim Weston and David Stirling (Ch.18 Good Reading).

Vancouver Island topographic maps have not been done in the 1:24,000 scale (7.5") that most U.S. hikers are so used to carrying. The largest scale available, 1:50,000 is comparable to U.S.G.S. 1:62,500 (15") maps. Also, be aware that extensive, accurate trail systems are not recorded on the B.C. topos. This means that even in large provincial parks like Strathcona and Cape Scott, you have to take the trail map and overlay it on the topographic map. The *Hiking Trails I, II, & III* do some of this for you in certain areas (II: Southern Vancouver Island; III: Central and Northern Vancouver Island). *The West Coast Trail & Nitinat Lakes Trail Guide* by the Sierra Club of Western Canada has trail maps with contour lines too. These are essential reading for travelers planning to hike the Island. But since they were prepared using the free time and work of mountaineers and climbers, they understandably do not cover all the backcountry you may want to see.

Solve the problem by contacting Maps B.C. (Ch.19, Maps). If you call or write them, they will mail you a **free catalog** of all the topographic maps for British Columbia, including Vancouver Island. Order maps before your trip, if possible, or stop by their office in Victoria. These maps are also available at some shops I have listed. A good compass and navigation skills are just as important on land here as on the water.

Clearly, backcountry travel on Vancouver Island, like traveling in Alaska or mainland British Columbia, demands skill reading the terrain as well as weather. One big advantage over the mainland or farther north is that there are no grizzlies to eat you or moose to chase you on trails. If you keep your head and practice basic survival techniques, getting lost may be only a temporary problem until you discover a landmark or hit a logging road. The old rule of hiking or climbing with a friend and telling somebody your plans applies in this country if you want rescue. You are expected to know about hypothermia, hyperthermia, CPR and wilderness emergency medicine if you go into the backcountry.

You should also carry the right equipment for what you plan to do, which ranges from nothing at all to a heavy pack of high

Stormr Olson and Andre Daigle after the West Coast Trail, at Port Renfrew.

angle ascent gear. Functional rain gear is essential. For backpackers, especially on the west coast, I would add a waterproof pack cover to any equipment list. This should be light, so you can stuff it in a sidepocket on nice days, bigger than the largest possible dimensions your pack can have with all the goodies inside, and pre-cinched with an elastic band, so it slips over top without tying. Taco colors like international orange or flaming pink beat forest green if you ever need a rescue helicopter to find you. Easy to make.

The search for the perfect hiking boot continues down through the centuries. Californians thought we had it licked when the industry came out with fancy "breathable-waterproof" creations that we all ran out and bought for a lot of cash. Most of them aren't waterproof or else they don't breathe. They trash pretty easily, and they generally don't give the ankle-leg support

71

you are looking for in a boot or you'd be wearing runners. So we're back to the best built leather hiking-climbing boot you can afford, that feels good on your feet, and that is broken in by the time you land on Vancouver Island. Unless you are skiing or on a snow trek, always include a pair of tennis shoes. For camp, yes, but also for those places where you have to go through mud or water and don't want to come out the other end with lug-soled boots that weigh 400 lbs.

In the Pacific Northwest, jeans are not an option for hiking, at least not for anything more serious than a few-kilometer, marked circle route leading back to your car. Or for hiking the beach near a road. Wet jeans that freeze their occupant, even in air temperatures above 0ºC, cause many tragedies in North America each year. The lightweight bombproof wool pants that all the mountaineering clubs have for years been advising you to buy at an army surplus store are getting hard to find. If you aren't hiking in heavy brush, a good option is hiking in shorts and packing wind-rain pants with side zippers and lightweight, warm bunting pants. If you have to brushbash, wear something that dries better than jeans and take a change of clothing. Goose down has the same drawbacks for jackets and sleeping bags--no warmth when wet. Shops on Vancouver Island as well as the mainland sell excellent synthetics. They carry most of the other gear you need for outdoor adventure.

There are over 40 provincial parks on big Vancouver Island and nearby islands. Some of these are quite large, like Strathcona and Cape Scott, or occupy whole islands, like Newcastle Island. Some are near towns or roads, like Goldstream and French Beach, yet provide great hike-in fishing, like Sproat Lake and Schoen Lake Parks. Many have historically significant features or host entertaining events. Brochures and maps for all these parks are available on the Island or from the Ministry of Environment and Parks (Ch 19). There are also many district and municipal parks, not to mention the extensive national park, Pacific Rim, which has 3 separate sections. Thousands of hectares of great unadvertised country challenge you. What to do?

First, realize it's the luck of the draw for everybody. An afternoon hike in a storm on the west coast might be kind of nifty or romantic. Three days inside a tent in an all-out blow on the side of some mountain followed by a retreat through avalanching snow is not funny. Every mountaineer's equipment should include one book or one place in your brain where you can escape when the weather closes in. Wallowing through Cape Scott mud in heavy weather has convinced more than one hiker not to like the park. But I breezed through in 3 days during dry summer weather. I have fine memories of that park, best of all, the north coast. So you will be affected by weather, bugs, and other lucky things.

Second, you can order the maps and read the books that describe hundreds of wonderful hikes and climbs, including ice climbs, on Vancouver Island (Chs 18 & 19). Third, consult the climbing organizations listed in Ch 16. Some are international. Particularly if you are an experienced climber or mountaineer, you can find a compatible partner who will be happy to show

French Beach, west coast Vancouver Island.

you his Island without charge. This is an outstanding way to make friends. Or self-equip to lead your own trip.

The best service I can do is to tell you about local guides and instructors who are not only competent but who will also give you a rich understanding of the area. Some of their tours may suggest self-guided routes to try. On north and west coast Vancouver Island--the wild places--outside is what there **is**.

Mike Henwood, who operates Mountain Line Tours out of Port McNeill, knows the North Island well: "A 6-hour trip goes into the Nimpkish Valley to the south end of Nimpkish Lake. You would go first to Anutz Lake then Little Hustan Cave Park, to Hustan Lake then on to Atluck Lake. From the shore here you can view Pinder Peak and many other peaks.

"We have full day tours that go into San Joseph Bay and Raft Cove on the northwest edge of the Island. Two-day trips go into Lowrie Bay and Sea Otter Cove. For this we could hike in from San Josef Bay Park and along the San Josef River to San Josef Bay then hike the trail up Mt. St. Patrick, down into Sea Otter Cove then across to Lawrie Bay to see the remains of the old settlement, the scenery, glass balls and what-ever else washes up on the beach.

"Another trip goes to Zeballos, perhaps to do some gold panning. The route from Nimpkish to Zeballos is cut right through a rock ridge. Builders had to have a perfect eye to do it. Both sides of the road are 200-300 ft cliffs straight up and down. All the way along in certain seasons huge waterfalls crash down.

"I took a group of Europeans from Belgium to Della Falls, south of Strathcona Park, for a 3-day camp. The approach is a 24-mile canoe run up Great Central Lake then 12 miles of hiking. We ended up staying 5 days right at the base of the falls! The falls enchanted these people. The highest falls in Canada--over 1500 feet high. These trips, including trips to the West Coast have to be reserved with us in advance.

"I took people from Chile hiking to San Josef Bay. It took 4 hours to do the hike in. The South Americans were photographing the ferns, moss on the sides of the trees, beautiful features of the rainforest that we who live here take for granted. They've got words this long [spreads out his hands] for our plants.

"If you hire a guide or ask us for trip advice, you should *listen* to what we say. One client went for a surprise swim. It took about 3 years off his life. We were near a fastwater river. He had a cup in his hand, and he wanted to get a drink of water. This is after we'd been hiking for about a half hour. We'd come into a glacier river. I said. "Take your pack off or your waist belt. Undo it before you go down there." He said, "I'm just going to get a drink." I said, "You should take it off or undo your waistbelt." As soon as he bent over, bang, he was in. He bobbed downstream in the white water then fought his way out, soaked. I tried to wash my hair in the same water that evening and just about froze my head.

"The Nimpkish Valley has some of the tallest trees on earth. I have seen pictures of trees there over 400 ft. high. Trees in the Nimpkish Island reserve are over 300 ft. tall and still growing. If they continue to grow, they'll be the tallest trees in North America, if not the world."

Myrna Boulding and her husband Jim started Strathcona Park Lodge over a quarter century ago: "The people who come here are bright, well educated, conservation-minded, curious, and not too concerned with appearances. We try to do things that are quiet, noninterfering with nature, mostly using your own energy to do--hiking and climbing, kayaking, board sailing, canoeing, swimming, reading and studying, birding or watching wildlife.

"We welcome seniors, especially groups that have their own program. It can't be just your run-of-the-mill bus tour. Seniors don't have to be extraordinarily athletic, but they have to be able to walk up and down hills for short distances, walk on gravel, and they can't be too unhappy when the lights go out at night. Ten years ago, that was a problem, but not anymore. Now, even if people have had a heart attack, medicine gets them out and moving. A prime advantage of Strathcona is the alpine atmosphere at a relatively low altitude.

"The Island's 5 climatic zones are all compressed. You can travel to dramatically different areas quickly. You can't get this kind of experience in the U.S. unless you go above 1800 m. We run courses that deal with the plant and animal life at the highest elevations we have here. Students can hike right up to examine them firsthand. Then our study passes down through all the bio changes until you're in the sea. Our students can hike through all the zones.

"In the winter, we have some of the world's best ice climbing. Very challenging mountains, even though you wouldn't expect that on an island. They go from 230 m up to almost 2200 m. Amazing. You don't take them lightly. You can't just sort of saunter up to Della Falls. We teach rock climbing well, and it's becoming more and more popular. Gareth Wood who followed Scott's route to the South Pole. He and 4 others are really good rock climbers and teachers. Peter Scott, one of the best known climbers in B.C., started here.

"When my husband and I started this center, we couldn't find people to help us with outdoor education and training. They didn't exist. So we started on the British model - canoeing, which was really kayaking, and rock climbing, and not a whole lot else. We hired people up from Outward Bound. John Jackson, who did centers in Great Britain and India, helped us get going. Two instructors from the U.S. helped us with experiential education. We evolved to present what we feel comfortable teaching and doing here. We were mainly interested in getting people interacting with the environment - out and about in it to protect it. Watchdogs for preservation, actually."

Guided hikes from narrated nature walks to 22-day mountaineering expeditions are available. This well known outdoor center conducts an incredible variety of programs on water, rock, and snow that go on summer and winter and bring people from all over the world. There is an apprenticeship program in outdoor leadership, youth and school group programs, Elderhostel programs, and all levels of rock climbing. Besides Strathcona Park itself, Lodge trips go to many parts of

Vancouver Island. For example, one great west coast backpacking trip goes out for 8 days to the isolated west coast of Nootka Island and explores the rugged wilderness there following the ancient trail originally used by Nootka Indians traveling to their summer hunting grounds. Write or call for their brochure: **Strathcona Park Lodge**, Box 2160, Campbell River, B.C. V9W 5C9, (604) 286-3122.

Pacific Rim is Canada's first national marine park. Its 3 separate units provide different but powerful experiences, all relating to the sea. Long Beach to the north is great beach hiking, surfing and camping. Parts of it are accessible by wheelchair. The middle unit--over 100 Broken Group Islands-- is reached by kayak or other boat (Ch 11). The south unit, the West Coast Trail, lies between Bamfield and Port Renfrew, a 72 km section named the "Graveyard of the Pacific."

Many vessels crashed on reefs there and sank. The *S.S. Valencia* from San Francisco that went down in a storm in 1906, killing 118 passengers and crew prompted the 5-year construction of a "lifesaving trail" along the coast there for ships in trouble. Modern navigation, communication, and rescue gear saw the end of trail maintenance until wilderness hikers began trying it. Now every year over 6000 people do the 6-8 day hike along the craggy shoreline. Parks has improved the trail in the last 10 years, but it is still remote and difficult. Before starting this trail, get current conditions from **Pacific Rim National Park** (Ch 19).

Long Beach, Pacific Rim National Park.

Wolf, Vancouver Island. -K. Atkinson, Ministry of Environment & Parks.

8. WILDLIFE: WHALES TO WOLVES
Gray Whale
(Eschrichtius robustus)

Sunny morning in Maurus Channel north of Tofino, the water is dark blue glass. A mature bald eagle poses about 20 m above the shoreline in a tall Vargas Island snag. Cameras click. A passenger says that is the first "in-the-feathers" live bald eagle he has seen. Annette Dehalt is the blond marine biologist piloting our 12-man Zodiac and lecturing about whales. She studied marine biology at Texas A&M, got her Masters in Oceanography at the University of British Columbia, and studied the feeding behavior and plankton diet of Alaskan humpback whales in Frederick Sound near Juneau. She took the Bamfield Station marine mammal course, given every 2 years. She studied gray whales and their feeding behavior.

"This village is called Opitsat on the southwestern tip of Meares Island. Coming closer to it, we're going to have to head around that red buoy. (Droning sound of the Zodiac in background.) According to archaelogical records, it has been there for at least 5000 years. If you ask the local Chief, he says 12,000 years. Who's to say? It is the oldest settlement on this coast. Once over 2000 Native Indians gathered there. In the summer, they spread out through the many harbors in family groups, then gather in more sheltered, protected harbors from the winter storms where they have potlatches and other social activities. Right now only about 200 people live there. They use Tofino as a base for grocery shopping and schooling. A speedboat taxis them back and forth. We're going to speed up now to get out to the whales and talk more once we're out there. (Engine noise, wind, and slapping water take over. We zip up our survival suits.)

"We're approaching Cowell Bay at the creek mouth on Flores Island, an area where in 1986 and early 87 there were half a dozen whales feeding, until they moved around Rafael Point.

79

Sometimes 1 or 2 come back here to feed, especially 1 juvenile. Altogether there are about 35 to 50 gray whales that spend the summer off west Vancouver Island. Of the 17,000 or so gray whales in this population, most travel all the way up to the Bering Sea and Arctic Ocean February-April for their summer feeding season. This year, during the last 2 weeks of March, historically the peak of spring migration, we saw hundreds of these grays blowing their way north. Towards the end of migration, what we call our "residents" come in. They don't go all the way up north but stay and do their summer feeding here. Then in the fall, in the November-January migration back down south, they join the rest of grays returning to Baja. Winter is their breeding season, spent in the lagoons of Baja, California. Traveling up to 16,000 km a year, the gray whales' Pacific migration is the farthest by any mammal.

"So let's just have a look in here (pulling closer to the island). The first thing you usually see of a gray whale is the spout - 2 to 3 m high or roughly twice a man's height -- that gives them away even at great distances. Sometimes they "fluke" their powerful tail with its 3 m span before they dive, leaving a Jacuzzi-sized slick on the surface. At closer range, watch for a never-ending, barnacle-encrusted back rolling into the waves for a dive. If we don't find anyone here, we'll go around the point and see if they're hiding there.

"We're dealing primarily with grays out here. There've been a few sightings of killer whales in this area, but they're seen much more often in the Inside Passage." Grays are common along the outer coast of Vancouver Island from the rocky headlands in Pacific Rim National Park, the West Coast Trail and Long Beach, to Cape Scott. Recently, they've been seen in the inside waters of Puget Sound, Boundary Bay, Georgia Strait and Johnstone Strait, and as far north as Rose Spit in the Queen Charlotte Islands.

"This large patch of white "bathtub foam' floating is phytoplankton. When the sun gets more intense in the springtime, photosynthesis goes wild -- the phytoplankton "blooms" -- and the zooplankton, small larvae, fish and crabs feed up the food chain, small fish to large fish. Some whales feed directly on the zooplankton, sea lions on the larger fish."

Does the sound of boats drive the whales off? "It depends. They have done preliminary studies with whales, observing them from rocks, and found that boats as far away as 400 m change the animals' breathing rate. Researchers who have worked for 15 years with the killer whales say that years ago when there weren't many boats, they rested a whole lot more. The resting behavior for pods has gone down. But they also got somewhat used to the boats because they let them approach closer. There are federal guidelines to protect marine mammals suggesting that boaters stay at least 100 m away, and let the rest of the closeness be the choice of the whale. Float planes are a real problem. When they dive below the legal 300 m altitude to take a closer look, their noise definitely disturbs the whales. You find differences between individuals and also varying reactions by the same whales on different days. If they're in a socializing mood they might come up right to the boat. If they want to feed or rest, they'd rather not have you within a mile. So you have to play it a little by ear. If I see a whale change his action frantically or dive longer, I try to lay off and look for a whale that's more approachable. I like to play conservatively before we scare them all away. I've had whales come up and rub against the pontoon of this boat and we could be petting them. You just never know. They're usually quite calm. They lie underneath the boat and check you out."

Whale Watching Guidelines

--Federal Fisheries Regulations: It is illegal to disturb or molest whales, dolphins, or porpoises. Be conscious of the effect of your actions on these mammals.

--Do not split up groups of whales, dolphins or porpoises.

--Do not disturb them while they rest motionless on the surface.

--Do not chase them, and avoid all sudden changes in speed or direction.

--Keep noise levels down -- no horns, whistles, shouting or

racing of motors.

--Approach whales from the side, not from the front or rear.

--When traveling with the whales, maintain a speed of 2-4 kts and do not alter speed abruptly. Traveling whales often surface for 3 or 4 breaths then dive for 3-5 minutes.

--If you are in a reserve, stay at least 300 m away from the whales. Only researchers are issued permits by the Park Programs Branch or the Department of Fisheries and Oceans to observe whales at closer range. Outside a reserve, you may approach to 100 m without a permit. Within 300 m, slow down and move forward slowly. Do not get closer than 100 m to a whale or dolphin. The animal may choose to approach closer than this; let it be his decision.

--When close to whales, let your boat drift silently. Cut the motor(s) and if possible lift it (them) out of the water. When leaving the site, start off smoothly and wait until you are 300 m away before picking up speed.

--Even if whale-watching isn't your primary objective, when traveling by boat in areas frequented by whales, exercise caution to avoid collisions. If you unexpectedly encounter whales, slow down, steer a straight course away from them, and wait until you are 300 m away before picking up speed.

--On board a plane, do not fly at an altitude lower than 300 m.

--Ecological reserves are not established for human recreation but for the benefit of wild species and their environment. Boaters should refrain from entering reserves when whales are present. Whales can easily be observed elsewhere.

The swells are about 3 m high. Ducks bob easily on the blue-black seatop. The weather is incredibly clear, waves breaking on the shorelines. One passenger remarks, "You look at a giant wave coming, you think, 'Oh my father I have sinned.' But though, the boat will do these spine-jolting crashes completely without warning." We ask a sailboat if they've seen any whales. They gesture out beyond the point. Against the oomph...oomph...oomph of the *Zodiac* hitting oncoming troughs, suits zip tight, collars stand up, ski caps are on. As we

Tuan crew watches killer whale, Johnstone Strait.

speed seaward, the boat's high bow shoves our bottoms back along both sides, packing us like 2 rows of sardines in a pontoon can. The cold air bites tears out of our eyeballs. We hang onto the side ropes, blinking around looking for whale blows. Annette, with her classic Norsewoman beauty, stands proudly behind the wheel, bravely driving us all through the rolling hills of water.

After a while we slow down to bail out the *Zodiac*, which has been taking a lot of waves over her bow. Annette fishes under our seats for a hand bilge pump. Everybody cooperates pumping the boat.

"Most baleen whales filter out the water either by skimming through it or some of them have expandable throats -- the humpback and blue whales -- and they look like feeding tadpoles underwater, taking even larger gulps of sea which they filter out through the baleen. The gray whale is unique in that it filters out predominately the mud. Mostly it uses shallow bays and bottom feeds. The less deep it has to dive, the less energy it uses to feed. Usually on the right side, with a little sucking motion the whale sucks material in through the jaw on one side and filters it out through the other side. What stays inside are small ghost shrimp, worms, arthropods, small crustaceans related to the beach hopper, crabs and the like. During the summer, they have to make up for the rest of the year when they hardly feed at all. At the rate of 300-400 kg per day, they add maybe 5 tons to their average 35 ton weight. While breeding down south, they fast. In the spring they come back skinny and begin gorging again."

A whale blows about 400 m north of us. Annette kills the engine, and we sit bobbing in the sea, holding our breaths for the sliding giant to surface again. He does, coming at us along with another smaller, possibly juvenile whale. We are above a 15 m shelf where underwater flow brings gammarid amphipods, mysid crustaceans, and polychaete worms within easy feeding range. The 2 whales spend about 5 minutes close to the *Zodiac..* They fluke. One rolls, curious around the boat. Then they move on.

"Wow, look at the jackfish! A small shark. He is probably eating what's being washed up through the gray whale's feeding.

"The grays form very loose social groups, whereas killer whales stay in a family unit for the rest of their life, the same animals moving together. We use the scars from the barnacles on the gray whales' backs to identify them. There is also some natural color in the skin. Since 1970, Dr. Jim Darling has studied grays, identifying them by photographing their natural markings. Gray whales all have unique white skin pigment patterns on a darker gray or black back. Photo-identification allows repeat sightings of individuals and provides the basis for accurate population estimates and behavior studies. We use photos to study grays, killer whales, humpbacks and dolphins. They are just now coming out with a book doing a full count of observed killer whales. They have a "mug shot" of each one. You can take that on a boat, go anywhere in B.C., and you'd probably recognize each whale.

"Japan and other nations have used "research" as the justification for killing whales. They've looked at dead carcasses for the last 200 years. You can learn so much more by observing living animals. There just aren't enough to keep slaughtering them. The gray whale in the Atlantic was extinct in the 17th Century, hunted by Basque whalers. In Japan, almost extinct. It's really only now along this coast of the Pacific that preservation has been promoted. Grays were almost extinct in the late 19th Century here. Recently, they discovered the breeding lagoons in Baja California. The gray whale wasn't protected here until 1946. It's done an amazing recovery from about 4-5000 estimated to almost the original stock size - around 17,000. It's very rare that an animal that high on the food chain can come back. They have typically a very low birth rate - in the case of the gray whale about one calf every 2 years. It's not like rabbits or mice that produce a lot. The only species naturely preying on the 15 m gray whales are killer whales and some large sharks, but it's almost negligible. Their births just make up for natural death. If you decimate a species like that, they can't usually bounce back."

Inter-Island Excursions, Box 393, Tofino, B.C. V0R 2Z0, (604) 725-3163. For more charters contact Tourism Association of Vancouver Island (Ch 16.)

Killer Whale
(Orcinus orca)

The killer whale is a familiar sight to mariners in southwest British Columbia. Canadian scientists Dr. Michael Bigg from the Pacific Biological Station, Dr. John Ford, Ian MacAskie, and Graeme Ellis of the West Coast Whale Research Foundation are pioneers in the study of free-ranging killer whales. In 1973, they began compiling photographs of killer whales in the protected waters around Vancouver Island and northwest Washington. Using naturally-occurring nicks, scars, and growth patterns on the dorsal fin, and the configuration of the lightly-pigmented "saddle patch" behind the dorsal fin, observers can identify individuals, track their movements, and monitor asso-ciations among the whales. The female's .5 m dorsal fin remains hooked or curved throughout her 75 year life, but the adult male's, over 1 m high, loses its curve and becomes bladelike. Killer whale flippers, shaped like rounded paddles, often show as the whale breaches and falls onto its side with a loud smack. The conical head has a large mouth lined with piercing teeth used for gripping and tearing prey, but not for chewing.

Like most other cetaceans, killer whales swallow their prey whole or in large pieces. They are skilled predators, their diet including nearly anything that swims. They eat turtles, ducks, and many kinds of fish and squid, as well as seals, sea lions, porpoises and whales. Pod preference depends on where they live: resident pods in British Columbia and Washington prey on salmon and herring. Antarctic killer whales regularly eat minke whales and seals. Although killer whales sometimes attack larger whales, they do not always kill successfully. Like wolves, killer whales hunt in a pack. Observers have seen several pods form a huge net-like ring in the water around salmon. The whales then take turns darting into the center to feed while the others keep the fish from escaping.

Northern Johnstone Strait is the core summer range of the northern group of killer whales in B.C. This group ranges from Campbell River to Prince Rupert and includes 13 pods with 160 whales. The southern group extends south into Puget Sound and Juan de Fuca Strait. It includes 3 pods (coded J, K, and L) with 75 whales, using as a core summer area Haro Strait near San Juan Island. Killer whales move into northern Johnstone Strait from July to October each year. Not all northern group whales are regular visitors here. Most sightings are of 5 pods with 50 animals. They spend the summer foraging along predictable salmon spawning routes in the Strait. When not feeding, they rest in tight-knit groups, socialize or play, or rub on steep pebble beaches known as the Rubbing Beaches in Robson Bight. Their cohesive family groups are apparent matriarchies.

Two "types" of killer whales live in B.C. waters: residents, described above, that live in fairly specific territories at least part of the year; and transients that pass through the entire area at irregular times, apparently ranging over a much larger region. The residents usually live in larger groups and eat fish. Transients live in smaller groups and eat mainly other marine mammals such as seals, sea lions and other whales.

Since a pod often disperses while foraging, they communicate by sound. The 3 basic sounds produced by killer whales are: 1. short, high-frequency pulses or clicks used mainly for echolocation; 2. somewhat lower-frequency "whistles;" and 3. pulsed "screams" which sound harsh and metallic to the human ear. Evidently each killer whale pod has a slightly different repertoire, or dialect, which may help pod keep the pod together when the ranges of 2 or more pods overlap.

Minke whales are also common in this area. These 6-8 m long baleen whales with a small dorsal fin are usually alone, feeding in tide rips or on "ballups" of small fish such as herring. Dall's porpoise, a small and extremely fast black-and-white porpoise, frequently feeds in tide rips. At a distance in open water, inexperienced observers mistake these for killer whales. Humpbacks, 12 m long baleen whales famous for their "songs" and surface acrobatics, once the most common large whale in B.C., are starting to make a comeback in north Island waters.

Stubbs Island Charters Ltd. -- Whale watching daytrips aboard the 17 m motor vessel *Gicumi* leave Telegraph Cove throughout the summer. Filled with observers from around the world, they cruise down Johnstone Strait looking for whales. *Gicumi* operators Jim Borrowman and Bill McKay talk with researchers to help locate the whales and have hydrophones to listen for the distinctive underwater calls of nearby whales. Telegraph Cove, B.C. V0N 3J0, (604) 928-3185.

Seasmoke Sailing Charters -- Out of Alert Bay, "Home of the Killer Whale" a few kilometers northwest, David and Maureen Towers sail their 13 m rigged cutter *S.V. Tuan*, also equipped with hydrophones, into Johnstone Strait and among the islands to give whale watchers the special experience of moving quietly with the orcas. Box 483, Alert Bay, B.C. V0N 1A0, (604) 974-5225.

Blackfish Expeditions -- From a private resort on Hanson

Island, multi-day whale and island cruise tours are available May through October. Box 45, Alert Bay, B.C. V0N 1A0, (604) 381-6455.

Contact the Tourism Association of Vancouver Island for more (Ch 16).

Sea Otters

In the reef-filled waters of northwestern Vancouver Island sea otters forage in kelp beds and bask in the afternoon sun. They are Canada's only sea otters, and though their numbers are climbing, they remain an endangered species. The 500 or so represent a fraction of the thousands that thrived on the Canadian coast before fur traders arrived. The cause of the sea otter's demise -- the last was shot in Kyuquot in 1929 -- was its smooth, silky fur. In 1969-72 there were 89 sea otters transplanted from the Aleutian Islands and Prince William Sound in Alaska to Checleset Bay on the northwest coast of Vancouver Island. Aerial surveys show them doing well and increasing.

The rocky shorelines and reefs of Checleset Bay are ideal sea otter habitat. The otters gather abalone and sea urchins in the shallows and stay on sheltered shores and in coves during storms. Accessible only by sea and air, the area receives few visitors. Among those are scuba divers exploring the colorful marine life of the Bunsby Islands in Checleset Bay. Divers, probably more than anyone, have seen dramatic habitat changes caused by the sea otters' foraging. Otters are red sea urchin gourmets, and the areas they harvest have almost no red sea urchins. Urchins limit kelp growth, so divers have found a tremendous variety of kelp and algae where otters took the urchins. Kayakers and sailors, visiting the Island's scenic west coast, come to Checleset Bay to see otters.

To watch Canada's sea otters in the wild, scan reefs and islands with binoculars or a spotting scope. After selecting a good viewpoint, approach quietly and stay hidden. Otters are cautious and will dive if you get closer than 100 m. The first sign of an otter is usually a beaverish face, 80% whiskers and 20% nose, peering over a kelp bed. They often drift on their backs, clutching pups or pounding rocks against oyster or clam shells on their chests, using the rock tools to open their food.

Underwater Life

Life under the water inside and around Vancouver Island is lush, definitely worth seeing. The Island's coastline is often rocky, plunging abruptly into the ocean. But in bays and on the sheltered side of spits and promontories water deposits sand and gravel, building beaches and ledges. The Gulf Islands and the west coast of Vancouver Island are similar. Many kilometers of rugged coastline supported Indians who harvested the rich intertidal life, leaving shell mound middens on nearly all the islands. When tides, that range over 4 m, travel through narrow passages, the turbulent waters may reach 16 kph. Here you can see exposed animals and plants that in other places require diving or dredging. A few are red sea urchins, anemones, sea stars, sea cucmbers, 6 varieties of shrimp and Dungeness crab as well as clams and oysters.

In summer filter feeders, such as clams and oysters, may not be safe to eat because of plankton called "red tide" that causes paralytic shellfish poisoning. When traveling, **ask** if there is a ban on shellfish in the area you plan to visit. There are bag limits for collecting shellfish.

North American Pacific salmon include 5 species -- chinook, coho, chum, sockeye, and pink -- all in the Greek genus meaning "hooked snout." All are anadromous, spending part of their lives in fresh water, then traveling to the ocean to grow and develop before returning to spawn in their original stream. The chinook, "king salmon" to sportsmen, is the largest, 2-14 kg, and lives 2-8 years. The pinks or humpies live 2 years and weigh 1.8 kg. The sockeye have bright red flesh and excellent taste. The naturally active, jumping coho thrill saltwater fishermen. Low-fat chum are ideal for smoking.

Commercial fishing uses 3 types of gear to harvest salmon on the Pacific Coast: 1. Gillnets (sockeye, pink, chum)--salmon swim into the floating web curtain, entangle their gills, and are individually removed from the gillnet as a drum retrieves it on the boat; 2. Purse seines (sockeye, pink, chum)--A fine-mesh net is set around a school of salmon, then drawn closed like a purse string trapping thousands of fish which are lifted on board; 3. Trollers (all 5 species)--6 stainless steel lines, hung 3 from each side of the boat, are weighted at the bottom with lures attached at intervals, 10-12 per line. Using power driven gurdies to pull in the lines, fishermen remove the salmon from each lure.

When Vancouver sailed along the B.C. coast buying fish from local Indians, Archibald Menzies, a naturalist on his ship identified the Pacific herring, one of the most abundant of the 250 fish species on Canada's west coast. Second only to Pacific salmon in value, the herring is prized for its roe, a delicacy exported to Japan. Other species are rockfish, bottomfish found from intertidal zones down to 900 m that are tasty but ugly and wildly colorful, and lingcod, not a true cod but prized for its size--up to 36.3 kg--and firm, mild flesh.

Birds
In his introduction to the Victoria Natural History Society's book:*The Naturalist's Guide to the Victoria Region* edited by Jim Weston and David Stirling (Ch 18. Good Reading), Yorke Edwards writes about "The Wild Side of Victoria:"

"Victoria is famous for its birds. Birders who have not birded west of the Great Plains will find a number of Victoria's commonest species to be new names for their lists. Glaucous-winged Gulls are everywhere as are Northwestern Crows, and Violet-green Swallows often outnumber other swallows. The Chestnut-backed Chickadee is a regular in parks and gardens. Pelagic Cormorants are always along rocky shores having islets on which they can loaf, and a sharp eye can usually find a Pigeon Guillemot in the tide rips near shore. Black Oystercatchers live year-round along some rocky shores. Gardens often have Bushtit flocks; the ear that knows their thin and incessant notes can find one from a moving car on a short drive through residential gardens. A flock is often within a block or two of the Provincial Museum (except at nesting time). Even downtown, watch the sky. A Bald Eagle, Raven, Double-crested Cormorant, or Great Blue Heron may be going over. On Government Street near Fort Street, note the easy presence of the Northwestern Crows in the town's busiest places. A sharp

Bald eagle found cold, wet and hungry in the bay at Coal Harbour, under care of conservation officer Lance Sundquist. -Ron Gebhard, courtesy

eye will also note stick nests in the trees planted in front of shops.

"Birding is never slow in Victoria. June is the slowest month, perhaps, because seabirds are reduced to those species that breed locally (but in mid-June begin to look for Rhinoceros Auklets in the tidal currents, gathering food to be carried to a colony on the American shore). Resident land birds, however, put on a good show in June, singing and nesting. Fall birds begin with sandpipers in the first days of July, and the passing parade builds up to the best birding of the year through September and October. Early winter is also good, especially after violent storms bring pelagics inshore; and all winter many wintering species on land and sea provide Canada's best winter birding in a region usually free of snow, at least near the sea. In winter, where I live overlooking rich and often turbulent waters, I can see 30 species in a day from my property with a little special looking and a lot of outdoor activity like cutting up beach wood. As an example, I saw 42 species on November 27th, including 3 species of loons, 3 of grebes, 3 cormorants, 8 ducks,

Bald Eagle, California Quail, 3 shorebirds, 5 gulls, 5 auks, Northern Flicker, and 9 perching birds. The following January 1st, I saw 26 species, and added 11 more on the 2nd.

"Victoria's winter show of birds is not widely understood. I know from experience that snowy Canada offers the fun of Redpolls and winter owls among other delights, but in autumn birds follow one another in abundance to Canada's main winter retreat for birds, the southwestern corner of British Columbia. Land and freshwater species come because fresh waters rarely freeze for more than a week or two (if at all), because little snow covers the food of ground feeders, and because abundant evergreen shrubs in gardens and dense thickets in wild places offer endless safe retreats. Seabirds come to famously food-rich waters that never freeze, Thayer's Gulls in dozens from the Arctic Archipelago, Brandt's Cormorants in hundreds from southern Californian waters, and many others from latitudes between. Follow the birds to Victoria, even if you live in California."

For outside adventurers who think birdwatching is for eccentric types wearing tweed and galoshes, you have a real surprise coming the day you are kayaking the Island shoreline and an osprey rockets into the water beside you to snatch a fish. More surprise when a bald eagle swoops over to take the fish away from the osprey. Birds are exciting wildlife to watch here, and their presence is a barometer of Island environmental health.

For more fun birding on Vancouver Island, I suggest you send for the cassette recordings: "A Field Guide to Western Bird Songs" arranged to accompany Roger Tory Peterson's *A Field Guide to Western Birds*. Even without the book, the birds are clearly announced. Once you hear your favorite species' calls, you will recognize them in a forest, village, cove or high mountain, so you can stop and look. Write: Cornell Laboratory of Ornithology, 159 Sapsucker Woods Road, Ithaca, NY 14850.

Vancouver Island Marmot
(Marmota vancouvernesis)

The rarest of all North American species, this marmot lives only on Vancouver Island. While collecting for the University of California in 1910, Harry Schelwald Swarth discovered the

The endangered Vancouver Island marmot. -A. Bryant.

marmot in mountains near Port Alberni. The next major sighting occurred in 1931 in mountains near Nanaimo. Today, they are still hard to see and study. They probably evolved from ancestral hoary marmots that crossed over to Vancouver Island on a temporary land or ice bridge during the Pleistocene times and became isolated here.

Members of the squirrel and chipmunk family, they are stout, dark brown furred with white nose patches and short bushy tails. They hibernate in the Island's deep wet mountain snowpack from late September until early May. This bright-eyed little mammal is endangered on its "island" mountaintops since it has such few, scattered colonies. If you discover a colony while hiking or climbing, watch without disturbing them, then report the sighting to the Fish and Wildlife Branch, Ministry of Environment in Nanaimo.

Big Land Animals

Perky jumpers, the **Columbian Blacktail** or coast deer that live on Vancouver Island move with a stiff-legged bounce as if on springs. These browsers select nutritional browse and need mature timber stands to survive, mainly in the forests of the Pacific wet slope. High rainfall encourages a rich growth of shrubs which, with lichens and blowdowns, provide ample winter feed. While they need both cover and browse, the

93

blacktail hunt shelter from cold winds and deep snow, sometimes choosing protection from bad weather over food growing out in the open and therefore starving. These shy animals have black tails, forked antlers, and scent glands.

The **Roosevelt elk** occurs in British Columbia only on Vancouver Island, having disappeared from the lower mainland 100 years ago. Bands exist in ancestral locations throughout the Island, from Cowichan north to Cape Scott, with herds occuring at Nimpkish Lake, Campbell River area, Nanaimo Lakes, Salmon River and White River, and major

Elk. Courtesy Ministry of Environment & Parks.

interior watersheds such as the Salmon, Nimpkish and Gold Rivers. These beautiful elk, the bulls weighing up to 1000 lbs and growing majestic racks each year, prefer parkland where clumps of conifers give shelter and where groves of deciduous trees linked by grassland or wet meadows provide browse, grasses for grazing, and herbs.

Found only in the Western Hemisphere, from northern British Columbia to Patagonia, the elusive **cougar** is the largest wild cat native to B.C. Adult males averaging 125 lbs, both sexes have great predatory skill -- can kill a 600 lb elk -- that has given these cats bad press. Rarely bothering humans, these agile hunters have a culling effect on sick or old members of deer herds and other prey. Island travelers who store camp food properly and do not leave very young children alone in the bush need not fear the legendary puma or mountain lion -- the cougar.

No grizzly bears live on Vancouver Island. All Island bears are **black bears**, their fur color varying from black or brown to cinnamon or blond. Weighing up to 600 lbs, they have long noses, no shoulder hump, maybe a white throat patch, and short claws for tree climbing. They eat everything from berries, grass, roots, stump grubs, herbs, fish, carrion, and small mammals to human food carelessly left on park tables or in tents. They are naturally shy of man but behave unpredictably when we enter their territory. You can bet a sow will aggressively defend her cubs. And if people feed bears, they lose their natural fear and become a dangerous nuisance.

Enjoy watching bears from a distance. Be alert for fresh bear sign: warm scat or droppings, fresh tracks, fresh tree scratchings, bear smell. If you meet a bear on a trail, don't run (he can outrun you). Back away slowly. But as Smokey warns U.S. travelers: "Don't feed the bears!"

Unless you are doing an authorized research project, do not feed any wild animals on Vancouver Island.

Wolves live on Vancouver Island. You will probably never see one. You will be lucky to hear one howl. *Canis lupus*, North America's largest wild dog, once had ranges from Mexico to Greenland. The wolf symbolizes unspoiled wilderness and freedom. Habitat encroachment and man have restricted wolves to very few ranges. Protected through provincial hunting regulations, British Columbia designates the wolf a big game animal.

Killer whale in Johnstone Strait.

9. HABITAT: FORESTS TO FISHERIES

The Haida people at Windy Bay, South Moresby: "We are out of balance with our environment...We must get back to the ethic that we are borrowing the land from our grandchildren...[at stake here is] the preservation of a world heritage...It will be to the everlasting shame to the people of this country if these places are destroyed."

The ethic that our race, the human race, must preserve our environment is a worldwide concern. Not only will it be to our shame if we fail to handle our resources correctly, but probably to our universal demise.

Travelers to Vancouver Island have a special chance to see virgin habitat -- marine, coastal rainforest, subalpine, alpine -- and learn what goes on here, such as the manufacture of oxygen and other important nutrients and the maintenance of living space for plants and wildlife. The Island is one of the few places where you can still see climax temperate rainforests. Lichens, mosses and ferns are abundant. Old growth trees that have never been logged may be over 1000 years old and over 8.8 m in girth. Western Red Cedar and Douglas Fir stand over 61 m (200 ft) high. Of course, virgin stands have the mixed species that provide food for a variety of wildlife. These are irreplaceable resources. Clean water and air are also an important part of the Island ecosystem.

Nesting sites for eagles and osprey are endangered by clearcutting near shorelines, leaving only a few trees for the birds to choose, with those snags and trees exposed to windfall. Changes in fertilization, shading of streams and soil, and silting of streams and seawater bordering logged areas affect life in the water too. How many times did I hear, with a shrug, "Oh, it's ugly now, but it'll all green up again." In fact, a flight over Vancouver Island reveals a mosaic of clearcuts as well as older logged areas that show severe erosion and the effects of monoculture. Extensive chemical use is necessary to control disease in single-species forests.

Vivacious Shari Bondy, Inter-Island Excursions, jokes and squints into the sun, enjoying her work. For 8 years, from the whale festival in March through October, she has been chartering her *Zodiac* for whale watching out of Tofino: "The environment is what makes Tofino. Meares Island is right on our doorstep. People come here to see wilderness, wildlife - whales, bald eagles, seals, tufted puffins, sea lions, aquaculture. The Tall Tree Trail is magnificent. You can't believe it until you see it. It's a virgin rainforest that hasn't been cleared. It's all bush, just like going into the jungle, vines hanging everywhere and lots of berry plants, bear, cougar, timber wolves still on the island.

"Chief Ben, I saw him this morning, he's in his late 80's, a direct descendant of Chief Maquinna, a renowned chief on the coast, [of] real fighters, warriers. Tofino is one of the few places in Canada where the natives and the white people live side by side and are fighting for a common goal - to protect our forests and our land. I really do believe that the land belongs to the natives. The natives still gather food and hunt, strip cedar bark, and they're working hard to sustain their culture.

"From the top bluff on Loan Cone, 721 m, Meares Island, you can actually see the curvature of the earth, the inlets, it's just incredible. It takes about 2 hours to walk up there from Kakawis. Tofino has an elfin charm created by the beautiful green mounds of islands. Now that the road is excellent, it's so easy to get here. You take the ferry, drive 3 hours from Nanaimo, and - BOOM - you're in Wonderland.

David Horst of Port Alberni: "I canoe the Stamp River system, which runs into the Somass, quite often. There seem to be a fair number of fellows in May going after steelhead and searun cutthroats. For a few weeks on the Stamp system, you may see 30 people in a stretch of 15 miles. The main pressure is in the fall, when the Springs (King) and the Coho come up. Just in the last few years, our hatcheries are performing real well, and the returns are good. Last fall, I took a fellow from Campbell River down a few times. Pools that were easy access to were crowded -- 4 or 5 guys in a 250 ft long pool. If I find that with the canoe, I

Looking for whales "outside" in an ocean of 2 m swells off Flores Island.

just move on.

"Nice lakes you can backpack to: Father & Son Lake, subalpine but got too popular; Labour Day Lake, I've pulled out 3-4 lb rainbow trout; Doran Lake, out toward Tofino, through the Taylor Valley, right on the top of a mountain at the 3000 ft. level, is a trophy lake; Great Central Lake has excellent rainbows, gang trolling deep. A place called the Powerhouse at the outflow of Elsie Lake is excellent flyfishing just before dark; McBride Lake, 2 hour hike, nice rainbows, not too crowded. A belly tube would be good there because the fish always seem to be a ways offshore. I've always done a raft. View Lake, just north of Great Central, is good too. They've logged just about to it. Nahmit Lake, where the river flows into the lake--they've got a logging road just about to it now(mostly big rainbow, steelhead and Dolly Varden). Henderson Lake is partially tidal. I went in there years ago before they logged. I have a little something for Henderson. I love the lake. The mountains all rise above it about 3000 ft straight up. At night, with the tremendous rain in there, all you hear is waterfalls. But now that it's logged, it's not quite the same feeling."

There is encouragement on the Island. While Strathcona Park

is still being mined, the shoreline around the marine preserve at Robson Bight will remain in virgin forest. As we go to press, the Province of British Columbia and the Nature Trust have bought some and will buy a total of 515 hectares (about 1250 acres).

In 1977, the Salmonid Enhancement Program (SEP) established a joint federal and provincial program hoping to restore the salmon harvest to earlier levels over the next 20 years. Fisheries and Oceans Canada and the British Columbia Ministry of Environment emphasize the 2 species of sea-run trout. SEP includes projects which maintain and upgrade the natural salmon habitat as well as construction and operation of man-made facilities for fish production. These include fishways, incubation boxes, spawning channels, rearing ponds, hatcheries, lake fertilization, and stream improvement.

Robertson Creek claims: "The Robertson Creek Hatchery supports the excellent fishing of the Barkley Sound area. Each year the hatchery releases about 10 million Chinook smolts. After 3-6 years in the ocean, they return as mature salmon averaging 24 lbs. The experienced angler can catch salmon from 40-50 lbs. Recently anglers have caught salmon over 60 lbs." SEP (Salmonid Enhancement Program).

Contacts:

Dept. of Fisheries & Oceans
Box 10, Port Hardy, B.C. V0N 2P0   (604) 949-6181
or Box 1328, Comox, B.C. V9N 7Z8   (604)
339-0431
or 816 Government Street Room 116
Victoria, B.C. V8W 1W9   (604) 388-3252

Pacific Biological Station

I recommend a visit to the Fisheries Research Branch in Nanaimo. Established in 1908, the station is the federal government's only fisheries research center on the west coast of B.C. The highly-respected center, with a staff of 200, does research in fish and invertebrate health and parasitology, fish culture and recruitment. The Station's research vessel, the *W.E.*

Demonstrating stainless steel and teflon "fish grader" of German design that efficiently sorts salmon by size with minimum stress -- to both the fish, which are not handled at all, and the human sorter, whose hands don't freeze as they do when grading by hand.

Ricker, is a 197-foot stern trawler, equipped to tow unmanned submersibles. It carries 22 crew and scientists, hydro-accoustic gear, computers, and wet and dry labs. Contact in advance to arrange tours:

Pacific Biological Station
Fisheries Research Branch
Nanaimo, B.C. V9R 5K6   (604) 756-7000
Habitat questions, comments? Contact:
Premier William Vander Zalm
Parliament Buildings
Victoria, B.C. V8V 1X4
Sierra Club of Western Canada
Box 202, Victoria, B.C.   (604) 386-5255
Western Canada Wilderness Committee
1200 Hornby St., Vancouver, B.C. V6Z 2E2

Board sailing. (North Island Gazette)

10. SAILING: BOARDS TO BOATS

"Wind's up on Nitinat. Let's go!"

Windsurfing

When it's sunny in Victoria there's sure to be wind, maybe a lot of wind, on lake and inlet waters from the south end all the way to Port Hardy. Boardsailing is the hot sport on Vancouver Island. Gear and technique are changing rapidly, from Jim Drake's 1969 paper at the American Institute for Aeronautics and Astronautics: "Wind Surfing -- A New Concept in Sailing" to a multi-million dollar industry pro-ducing dozens of boards and rigs for the awestruck surfsailor to choose from. There are even 5 or 6 different words for this Olympic sport.

Surfsafety:

--Always wear a P.F.D. In Canada it's the law.

--If doing radical aerial jumps, wear a surf helmet.

--Know your equipment and check it out (including a leash).

--Know marine navigation, right of way, and self rescue.

--Always stay with your board.

--Wear appropriate clothing (wet or dry suits in Canada, plus sunscreen, shoes, & sunglasses with keepers or tinted contacts).

--Learn local sailing hazards.

--Let someone on shore know your sailing plans.

Hypothermia, the big watchword: Watch your body & buddy for signs.

Launching, the big chill: If it's an aerial (e.g. jumping from a rock) entry, preplan your takeout.

Fun places to boardsail on Vancouver Island:

Elk Lake (On Hwy 17 fifteen minutes north of Victoria)--Great place for beginners -- you can acquire all the basic skills in 10-12 hours of guided practice. Easy beach entry & warm up in the sun, dry land & water instruction, rentals, refreshments nearby, quick access when weather changes & wind comes up or to check out new equipment. Parking can be a problem. Expect crowds on weekends, holidays & breezy summer afternoons. Good access for photography: still or video.

Cowichan Lake (Hwy 18 west of Duncan, Honeymoon Bay)-- Good beginner area, rentals, paved road access. Complete resort facilities.

China Creek (China Creek Marina, 13 km south of Port Alberni)--Large rigging area, solidly constructed windbreak fence, outdoor shower for cleaning equipment & refreshing tired surfers, playground for kids who don't yet appreciate the finer points of windsurfing, host for major world class competition. Lessons & rental equipment. Ask locally about lakes, such as Sproat & Great Central.

Strathcona Park Lodge (Upper Campbell Lake, 45 km west of Campbell River on Highway 28 to Gold River)--At the junction of 3 mountain valleys, Upper Campbell Lake warms up in the summer & you can almost set your watch by the winds. Instruction & rentals: start by getting the feel of the sail while still on the dock, then graduate to a protected bay. Once you have the skill, sail back & forth across the lake with an instructor to encourage you & teach the finer points of board-sailing. Special holiday & youth group packages to other Island destinations. Full services resort.

Nimpkish Lake (On Hwy 19, 10km south of Port McNeill)-- Sometimes very high winds, home to seals, saltwater in lower/north end of lake, freshwater in upper/south end. If camping, drive into south end via logging road west of Woss. Great backcountry makes this area wonderful for a longer trip including hiking, canoeing, wildlife watching, etc.

Nitinat Lake (Logging road access west of Lake Cowichan, about 2 hours drive from Victoria)--Beautiful, deep tidal lake moderately salty, unsuitable for drinking, generally poor sports fishing. Strong westerly winds. Thermal winds consistantly start around mid-day & increase to good afternoon shortboard conditions. Water is relatively flat, warm. Weekend or special instruction by Victoria shop; rentals, lessons with & without video playback, fun races & slalom buoys set up for gybing practice, family games, swimming & hiking, nature photography, B.B.Q.'s. MacMillan Bloedel Campsite next to Indian Reserve has 12 sites, pit toilets, tap water, picnic tables & boat launch.

Long Beach & Tofino (130 km west of Port Alberni on Hwy 4)-- Long Beach has the best surfing, a 20 km stretch of it, in British Columbia. Incredible beaches. Tofino offers 2 beaches within walking distance--Mackenzie & Chesterman. Camping & full services for the entire family. Many other sports & sights nearby.

Strait of Georgia (Qualicum Beach to Ladysmith)--Many launch areas, good beach camping, local instruction.

Cook Street (Victoria headlands between Clover Point to the east & Holland Point to the west)--A short, steep wave chop, 25-30 kt winds, & brilliant sunshine are common in spring & early summer. Exciting slalom racing & race across Juan de Fuca Strait from Victoria to Port Angeles organized by local shops. Sailors prefer to rig up, top then go down cement path to turret, with spiral stairway leading to beach. Swells 1-3 m high make brutal beach break; crucial to time your entry or break will grind you up. Prevailing side shore wind enables speeding off on a

Victoria to Port Angeles sailboard race.

fast reach. Farther out pick up stronger winds. Swells can give exciting air time. Avoid kelp beds. Stay upwind of Clover Point or 6 kt rip tide will suck you into next bay.

Boardsailing shops are at Strathcona Park Lodge, Honeymoon Bay, Nanaimo, Port Alberni, Tofino, and Victoria.

Hang Gliding & Parasailing

Hang glider pilots soar the thermal updrafts generated by the cliffs at Cook Street, Victoria. East side bays, inlets & the Strait of Georgia offer unlimited opportunities for parasailing.

Sailing

David and Maureen Towers, skipper and wife-mate of Sea Smoke Sailing Charters (Ch 8. Wildlife ...) serve morning coffee and biscuits as we get underway out of Alert Bay. David is a former logger. He has 16 years on the water booming, sorting, and scaling logs. He loves the outdoors, the freedom of the wind and water. He saw the future and wanted to get out of the logging industry, so bought this boat. Maureen is a nurse at the hospital in Alert Bay, often working graveyard shifts in the emergency room. They met while trekking in Australia.

The *S.V.Tuan* -- Salish for "facing the sea" -- is a 13 m rigged cutter appointed with Honduran and New Zealand woods and designed for year-round sailing. The boat's tiller is a meter long piece of Island yew wood--golden, dense, and heavy. I man the tiller while David raises the sails. I instantly dream of skippering her as we nose south into John-stone Strait.

Towers respects his boat: "Facing into the wind, I put the sail up quick, then the boat will always come into the wind. You'll heel off the wind, but she'll always right herself into the wind if I leave the tiller alone.

"I had just come to this area in 1970. I am in a little 16 ft. runabout that I just bought. I am out here in the islands first thing in the morning and the fog bank rolls right in like pea soup, kind of scary. You just keep close to the shoreline cause you can't see anything around Oosh!, Whish! -- 20 whales right around me. My heart was up in my mouth. I was afraid they were going to crunch my boat. Now killer whales seem so

106

David Towers furling sail on the *Tuan*, Johnstone Strait.

friendly, wild and free. But then their reputation...the big bulls with their massive dorsal fins. It blew my mind. I was 19. That was my first experience with killer whales."

The first day looking for killer whales on the *Tuan*, we get skunked. The whales have gone somewhere else. But the passengers are so friendly, the homemade quiche, thick soup, and salads so wonderful, the day so gorgeous for sailing, that everyone on board is happy. In the afternoon we cruise off an island with granite cliffs and watch kayakers practice rock climbing above the water. At a tiny forested island, we slip next to a fisherman's house floating on a log dock and celebrate the afternoon with the Towers' Devonshire tea--freshbaked scones, home-made jam, and handwhipped sweet cream. Tomorrow we will sail with the whales.

Order **tide tables and charts** for the waters you plan to sail from the Canadia Hydrographic Service (Ch 19. Maps). For west coast sailing around Vancouver Island: Pacific Yachting's *Cruising Guide to British Columbia Vol. IV, West Coast of Vancouver Island*, Cape Scott to Sooke including Barkley Sound by Don Watmough (Ch 18. Good Reading).

M.V. Uchuck III

We are riding a 41 m ex-American minesweeper out of the Gold River dock in Muchalat Inlet. Freight and passenger stops determine where the *Uchuck* will stop en route. Nootka Sound Service Ltd. is the cheapest way to get heavy freight out to the west coast on this part of Vancouver Island. She runs with a crew of 5, this week: Keith Machin, Captain; Glen Pollock, Mate; Dennis and Mike Bye, Engineers; Angela O'Keefe, cook. Days are long for the crew, starting before light and running past 8 pm.

Watching the bright reflection of the wake, I listen to the engines beat. Acrid pulp mill smells fade with the fog into the far end of the fjord. Every crew member works with his hands -- steering, shifting cargo, minding the engines, serving meals -- to supply mail and goods to people living along the Island's west coast. Like acting, the crew's performance is so good that I start realizing "the play's the thing." Mike one-handing the grappling hook for a thrilling ride over the water from the dock to the deck. Keith doing such a perfect docking maneuver that everybody claps. Glen driving the electric boom to raise a large forklift and deposit it gently in the ship's hold. For 2 days here on the *Uchuck III*, you can lean back, put your feet up and watch Island bays slide by, eat when you feel like it, and best of all watch the crew work! I am fascinated by the passengers' collective interest in watching the crew. Crewmembers don't give each other commands. While working, they rarely speak. Even though they rotate tasks, each knows what the other will do.

Keith's interest in kayaking stems from kayakers aboard the *Uchuck*, all friendly and having a good time: "Last trip we had a group from Washington State, older people, really organized canoers. They had special fittings to hook the kayaks together side-by-side rigidly. They had masts with sails." Past Plumper Harbour, we go through the narrows of Kendrick Arm. Keith says sometimes on a black night, passing through here, he has to slow the boat to less than half speed and keep a sharp eye out

Uchuck III delivering cargo en route to Kyuquot.

to get through. Bald eagles perch in snags watching the boats. Two bears play on a beach. At one dock we drop off boxes of ice cream, apple pie, milk and eggs.

After docking in Kyuquot harbor at dusk, the *Uchuck* crew tells sea stories around a few beers. Dennis Bye really gets into it, talking about big weather in the 1960's, broken moorings, fierce, driving gales that drilled the wheelhouse: "We were headed for Victoria on the outside (open ocean). The winds were 60 kts and gusting. We turned around and went back. The seas start damaging the ship when it gets that heavy. Storms don't very often stop the *Uchuck*.

"One time we found an expensive, hi-tech boat somebody had

apparently tied to a log. The whole thing just floated off! Another time a guy was having some trouble. His boat was moored near him, lost its rudder. He'd built a signal fire on the beach that you could see for miles. We started over that way, and he got real excited, worried that we wouldn't see him. Well, he fired off a signal flare. It went straight through his boat's rigging! Then he went to light another. I was afraid he'd send one through the rigging again before we could get to him!"

Go west aboard the *M.V. Uchuck III* (reservations needed): Nootka Sound Service Ltd., P.O. Box 57, Gold River, B.C. V0P 1G0, (604) 283-2515.

Marinas & Charter Boats

For marina and charter boat information, contact the Travel Infocentres nearest your destinations (Ch 16.) or contact the **Tourism Association of Vancouver Island** (Ch 16.).

Getting it started in Ucluelet Inlet.

Gill netter and otter trawler in Friday Harbor, San Juan Islands, from Washington State Ferry to Sidney, B.C.

West Coast Whaling Canoe carved by Chief Charlie Jones (1974).

11. KAYAKING & CANOEING

The free, intimate, exciting way to explore Vancouver Island water is by kayak or canoe. Time is your own. Watch an osprey nest for hours. Paddle fast in swift water. Meet whales. Age is no barrier and you will have the most incredible adventures of your life.

John Dowd's kayak: "...a silent, responsive craft, with clean lines and one of the most basic forms of propulsion there is: a boat which impels the lone paddler into reverent harmony with the sea and enables the explorer to probe where no other vessel can reach: so silent the photographer or hunter can slip up to wild animals without ever disturbing them, and so rugged and indomitable it can ride out gales on the open sea."

Sizes and shapes range from short, single-man models designed for inland lakes and streams to the ultimate in custom seaworthiness: George Dyson's 14m, 6-man, 3-masted *Mount Fairweather*, with detachable outriggers and weatherproof Perspex domes. An outcrop of this class of vessels is the open-decked, pointy-ended craft U.S. paddlers call a canoe, usually less maneuverable than a kayak. Most travelers interchange the terms canoe and kayak. You can rig a sail on just about any kayak; some stock models have this feature already built-in.

Sea and weather:

--Dress for the sea. Ocean temperatures in the Vancouver Island area average between 5º-15ºC (41º-59ºF). We're talking hypothermia, even in midsummer. Daytime may be sunny and warm, but when you're out there taking a beating from the waves your body temperature can drop in a flash. Especially for off-season expeditions, outside July-August, take extra protection for your hands and feet. You are totally helpless if you cannot paddle or walk. Wool works, but I like Patagonia's Synchilla pants and jackets.

--Go with the flow. Summer weather is nicest. But more people travel then too. You can kayak March through

November if you realize spring or fall storms can be serious. Watch the barometer. Watch satellite weather maps and listen to local forecasts. Gear up for winter conditions. Don't be too proud to turn back. Don't "**Have To Go**" anywhere.

--Pay attention to experts. The books I mention here and competent instructors are good sources. Water*proof* rain gear is still the best. Tools, repair kits, and survival gear: *Use* them before you go on a trip. *Don't lose* them.

Canoeists Jane Rutledge and Neil Gray, training consultants from Vancouver on honeymoon, riding the *M.V. Lady Rose* to the put-in at Gibralter Island in the Broken Group: "We're taking 20 liters fresh water for a week. Food is mostly boil in a bag, some freeze dried. Weight is a factor; we are carrying about 200 lbs total. We have a crab trap and hope to catch some Dungeness Crab. I'm going to eat some goose barnacles; I understand they taste like chicken. We brought extra seasonings. The one fresh water lake on one of the islands is kind of rough to get to. We've got a mountain tent with a fly, all the standard stuff. And a solar shower. We have PFD's. In the Broken Group we plan to keep relatively close to shore. Water on the West Coast is pretty cold, and hypothermia is a factor. This time of the year you've got about 20-30 minutes with the gear we've got, but we should be able to get to shore in that time. We've got compass and map, flares, water-proof matches, our survival stuff is spread out over several packs. If the majority of it floats, we've got things spread around in doubled plastic bags.

"I plan to fish, but I don't know if I'd want to tie into a salmon in a canoe! It would depend upon the size and which direction he's heading. Hopefully, I can paddle to shore with one hand. On the Sunshine Coast 3 years ago, I was in a 14 ft. aluminum on a Hardy split cane fly rod, mooching with live herring, drift fishing. I caught one I couldn't fight. All I could do was hold the pressure against him. For 3 hours he towed me around. I'd gain a little bit, he'd gain a little bit. I finally got him up to the surface. He was right on his side and I thought, you're damn near as tired as I am, fella!"

Neil and Jane couple of months later: "It was the most beautiful spot to go just to do *nothing*! The weather was gorgeous the whole week. We came back as brown as berries, saw the majority of the Broken Group, had an absolutely fantastic, tranquil time. We caught the *M.V. Lady Rose* at Gibralter Island again coming back. When you guys dumped us off at the dock and drifted into the wilderness, we threw all our gear into the canoe, jumped in and got about an hour into our trip. I'm sort of mentally setting up camp in my head, and I say, "Jane, where are our sleeping bags?" We had left our sleeping bags on that float because there was so much gear with other kayakers getting off. We had to turn around and paddle back.

"We spent our first 3 nights at Gibralter Island. The first night we got back too late to go all the way over to the other side again, so we set up camp and had the whole place to ourselves for 3 days. We didn't catch any crabs in the trap, just starfish. But we did find a shallow tidal flat where we could just flip the crabs out with one of the canoe paddles! Crabs do take quite a bit of white gas to cook, and we found we didn't have as much fuel as we could have used. Lots of people did fish. Fellow from Seattle in a camp next to us on our 4th and 5th nights caught himself a couple of cod every day.

"Paddling around sightseeing we saw killer whales, seals, osprey, eagles, a deer on one of the tiny islands who was tame as could be, lots of mink. *Unreal* sunsets.

"Next time, we would use kayaks instead of a conventional, open-decked canoe. The canoe was wetter and harder to maneuver. We had strong westerlies that made difficult paddling. We set up base camps on a couple of different islands and made day trips out from there rather than touring around with our whole load. We saw 5 women in their 50's and 60's with single kayaks. One woman was making her 3rd trip in the Broken Group.

"Besides the advice on adequate fuel, water and plenty of toilet paper, if you want to head west, do it before 10 am, before the westerly winds rise. It's a pretty hard paddle. We did it one

115

day and regretted leaving so late in the morning. If you want to go east, leave after 10 am and get the free ride. We saw kayaks with sails and canoes with jury-rigged sails. Saw one guy in a kayak with a parasail, just leaning back and drifting along.

"There are pit toilets on the islands. We brought our garbage out with us. People are careful. We found very little litter, no debris from boats. And a 40 oz bottle of scotch won't last 7 days!

"We'd highly recommend this trip to anybody who likes the out-doors and peace and quiet. The sunsets are right out of this world!"

Open Water Kayaking/Canoe Trips

The following trips are all described in detail in John Ince and Hedi Kottner's book: *"Sea Kayaking Canada's West Coast"* (Ch 18. Good Reading). Other excellent sources: John Dowd's *"Sea Kayaking"* and Bruce Obee's *"The Pacific Rim Explorer"*. I recommend you read these in advance. **Important: You must have required skills, safety and navigation gear for these adventures.** Outstanding kayak/canoe training centers operate on Vancouver Island, in-cluding Strathcona Park Lodge. Getting a tide table before you go and studying it can suggest a paddling schedule that will give you several knots of free speed and save paddling against the strong currents in many passages.

Shipping traffic is heavy in Johnstone Strait, Discovery Passage, Haro Strait and Active Passage. Feeling like a cyclist on an interstate, you can find yourself facing ferries, cruise ships, self-propelled log barges, and tugs with 1-3 barges behind them, all limited to the center of the channel. They can appear suddenly around a bend just as you're avoiding a 3 ft. deep whirlpool. Watch carefully, cross the shipping channel quickly without staying in it, and don't be out there at night or in the fog (when you don't show up well on their radar and all you can hear is booming foghorns on all sides).

Gulf Islands--South
Access: The put-in point is either of 2 places in Sidney: 5 km south of Swartz Bay or 26 km north of Victoria off Hwy 17. The first spot is a beach south of Sidney by the Anacortes ferry, the second is in town at Roberts Point.
Description: This trip takes you through both protected and open waters with some crossings over 2 km in length. There are a number of islands to explore and 3 marine parks for camping. The best time of year

Near Gibralter Island

to travel these waters is April to June when all the flowers bloom. Hazards here are the busy ferry terminal and small craft traffic between the terminal and Sidney.

Chart: 3441 Haro Strait, Boundary Pass & Satellite Channel

Gulf Islands--North

Access: There are several put-in points for this route: on Vancouver Island they are Yellow point and Boat Harbour, both located between Nanaimo and Ladysmith; the northern end of Saltspring Island; Retreat Cove on Galiano Island; the south end of Gabriola Island; and Thetis Island.

Description: This trip will take you through the relatively flat waters of Trincomali Channel, Georgia Strait with its choppy water and the swift tidal currents of Porlier Pass and Gabriola Passage. There is developed camping at Pirates Cove on DeCourcy Island. Beaches are scarce, so undeveloped camping areas are hard to approach. The trip should take anywhere from 2 days to a week. There are plenty of Island chains to explore with their cliffs, sculptured rock and petroglyphs.

Chart: 3442 North Pender Island to Thetis Island, 3452 Thetis Island to Nanaimo

Kayaking

Discovery Islands

Access: There are several put-in points for this trip: on Vancouver Island use Rock Bay, about a 60 km drive from Campbell River. By taking the ferry from Campbell River to Quadra Island you can put-in at Heriot Bay, Village Bay or Granite Bay. Another ferry from Heriot Bay to Cortes Island gives access to Whaletown and Coulter Bay as put-in-points.

Description: This trip takes you through protected, narrow channels and distances between islands are short, so there are no difficult passages. But due to tidal rapids, whirlpools and overfalls, which are dangerous to small craft *except at slack tide,* only adult paddlers with experience interpreting tide and current tables and marine charts should try this route. Experienced local advice is invaluable. Best time of year is March to October. The waters are rarely crowded, except in Discovery Passage between the islands and Campbell River. There are many cobblestone beaches and low bluffs for camping. Enjoy hiking around the various old homesteads on the islands.

Chart: 3594 Discovery Passage, Toba Inlet and Connecting Channels, 3566 Johnstone Strait (Eastern Section), 3524 Bute Inlet, Tidal current Chart No. 23 for Yuculta - Dent Rapids.

Western Johnstone Strait

Access: Telegraph Cove and Port McNeill are both excellent put-in points. Alert Bay is a great put-in reached by taking the ferry, with or without your car, to Cormorant Island.

Description: Orca whales are the big attraction for kayakers here. Robson Bight and Blackfish Sound have the largest concentration of orcas found. Stay out of the rubbing rocks area in Robson Bight to protect whale habitat. Hazards are the heavy marine traffic and wakes caused by the boats. There are many camping beaches on the Vancouver Island side of Johnstone Strait. If you plan to cruise in the islands, starting in Alert Bay eliminates the span across Johnstone Strait. The top of Cormorant Island has a campground with awesome views across the Strait and north.

Chart: 3659 Broughton Strait, 3568 Johnstone Strait (Western Section)

Cape Scott to Brooks Peninsula

Access: Two put-in points for this route are San Josef River near the Cape Scott Park Boundary and Winter Harbour. Reach both via unpaved road from Port Hardy to Holberg, then follow the signs to either put-in.

Description: This route takes you past some of the most interesting coastline on Vancouver Island and challenges advanced kayakers. The entire area often has heavy swells and gale force winds. The best time to take this trip is June to September. Allow at least 3 days for a partial trip to 14 days for a complete round trip. There are many deserted sand beaches for camping, though you usually land through the surf.

Chart: 3617 Quatsino Sound, 3624 Cape Cook to Cape Scott,3680 Brooks Bay

Kyuquot Area

Access: Fair Harbour is the put-in point. Starting at Campbell River, drive north on Hwy 19 for 160 km, then just before Nimpkish Lake turn west on the logging road to Zeballos and on to Fair Harbour. Since you are using a logging road, check with the Regional District of Mt. Waddington in Port McNeill about road restrictions or closures.

Description: Inside the Sound the waters are sheltered. Between Kyuquot Sound and Bunsby Islands, you are in open ocean. Be aware of hazards such as heavy seas, frequent fog, and at high tide a chain of reefs that are just below the water level. There are many sand and pebble breaches for camping. Abundant wildlife in the area includes bears and wolves (suspend food high in trees or cache it away from your camp).

Chart: 3682 Kyuquot Sound, 3683 Checleset Bay

Nootka Island

Access: Tahsis Pulp Mill at the head of Muchalat Inlet is the put-in. Reach via Gold River on Hwy 28. Option to see more: reserve space on the *Uchuck III* going or returning to shorten the long paddle down/up Tahsis Inlet.

Description: The open ocean is subject to heavy swells. Only experts should paddle there. Visit Strange Island, Jewitt Cove, Bligh Island, Resolution Cove, Friendly Cove and many other places full of Vancouver Island history. Read about the area before you go, and be amazed at how the first explorers did it. There are a few deserted Indian villages and at least 2 excellent totems. Beach camp on the exposed coast and use abandoned logging camps along the inside route. The driest time to go is July or August. You can enjoy a brief 4-6 days. If you circle Nootka Island, allow 2 weeks.

Charts: 3662 Nootka Sound to Esperanza Inlet, 3663 Esperanza Inlet, 3664 Nootka Sound

Kayaking

Clayoquot Sound

Access: Tofino -- the public wharf or any beach -- is the put-in. Drive to Tofino on Hwy 4 from Parksville.

Description: Paddlers have 2 possible routes: the protected inside passage with many islands to play around or the open ocean with exposure requiring sea skill. You can take a circle route and experience both. Hazards are chiefly the heavy boat and floatplane traffic at Tofino. April through August is the best weather for enjoying this route. If planning an extended stay at Hot Springs Cove, brace yourself for weekend crowds. Take light hiking boots for exploring on Meares Island, Lone Cone (great views, especially on moonlit night), and Flores Island. Study the local history, including recent environmental battles, before you go. Plenty of camping on beautiful beaches along both routes.

Charts: 3640 Clayoquot Sound, Lennard Island to Estevan Point, 3648 Clayoquot Sound (Northwest Section), 3649 Clayoquot Sound (Southeast Section)

Barkley Sound

Access: Choose from 4 major put-ins depending upon your skill, time, weather, and what you want to see. The most popular, therefore most crowded in summer, is to board the *M.V. Lady Rose* at Port Alberni (need reservations), and she will drop you off and/or pick you up at one of the Broken Islands. You can drive 90 km past Port Alberni to Kennedy Lake, turn southeast on the logging road to Toquart Bay put-in. If you are an experienced sea kayaker, put-in at Ucluelet or Bamfield.

Description: Protected by the outer islands, the Broken Group Islands are perfect for family or leisure paddling. Many sea caves and wildlife in the air, on land, and underwater are a real treat. Campspots are plentiful. There are 3 Indian Reserves in the Broken Group -- on Effingham, Keith and Nettle Islands. These are private, legally protected lands, so do not trespass. April through October are best, but July and August are very crowded. Do not burn wood; bring stoves. Pack out all your garbage. Hazards are sailboats or speedboats and other motored craft enjoying the islands. The crossing from either Ucluelet or Bamfield is for experienced kayakers only.

Chart: 3670 Broken Group, 3671 Barkley Sound, 3638 Broken Group
Information on the Broken Island Group:
Pacific Rim National Park, P.O. Box 280, Ucluelet, B.C. V0T 3A0

M.V. Lady Rose, P.O. Box 188, Port Alberni, B.C. V9Y 7M7 (reservations needed, kayak & canoe rentals available), (604) 723-8313

Whitewater Kayaking & Canoeing

The whitewater river season on Vancouver Island is brief but can be exciting. For more information, read Betty Pratt-Johnson's book: *"Whitewater Trips for Kayakers, Canoeists & Rafters on Vancouver Island"* (Ch 18. Good Reading).

Outdoor Club of Victoria, P.O. Box 1875, Victoria, B.C. V8W 2Y

The canoe. -by Tony Sayle. (Strathcona Lodge)

Sea kayak.

Crosscountry skiing Mt. Washington. (Tourism Comox Valley).

12. SKIING

Where in the world can you ski powder or telemark a trackless slope in the morning, drive a few kilometers to play golf in the sunshine, fish, dive or windsurf in the afternoon? **Winter is really the "high" season on Vancouver Island.** Skiing this beautiful Northwest destination is affordable, exciting, and relaxing fun. Affordable because off-season rates apply at many hotels, motels, and resort lodges on the Island. Also, lift and track fees are as low as any in North America. The skiing is exciting with a wide range of slopes along the Island's mountain backbone. Being here relaxes you in a healthy way -- friendly people, little traffic, clear air, good access.in short, no hassles. Children are welcome. Area staff are ready with programs for them. So your whole family can have a wonderful ski holiday.

Mt. Washington Ski Resort

The Mountain: Mt. Washington's is 1608 m (5260 ft) high. The Blue Chair takes you to the mountain's peak and a spectacular 360º view. To the north is Campbell River and Discovery Passage. To the east you can see Powell River and the mainland mountains. To the south beyond the Comox Valley, Denman and Hornby Islands. To the west Comox Lake, the gap to Port Alberni and the Golden Hinde, the highest mountain on Vancouver Island. In the lee of Pacific storms, the mountain develops deeper snow than any other ski area in Canada, yet you often ski in blue-sky weather. The mountain has 24 runs, beginner to expert. CSIA ski school: lessons and terrain for all skier levels including children.

The Lifts: Two double chairs; Two triple chairs; One handle tow. Alpine Lodge: Rental/repair, ski shop, dining and first-class ski school plus evening apres ski activities including a full bar with live entertainment. Kids Brigade Room offers child-minding for 2 years and up. General store & liquor store in the village.

Crosscountry Skiing: 30 km of triple-track-set groomed trails offer routes for all levels of nordic skiers. Explore the rolling expanse of Paradise Meadows, Helen McKenzie and Battleship Lakes and discover vistas including Mt. Albert Edward.

The Nordic Lodge: Located at the base of the Red Chair, the Nordic Lodge offers fresh-baked pastries and lunch plus ski rentals and accessories. Certified instructors teach private and drop-in lessons.

Forbidden Ski Resort

Forbidden Ski Resort lies half in the Wood Mountain Ski Park and half in Strathcona Provincial Park, the oldest in British Columbia. People have skied Forbidden since the 1920's, making it one of the oldest ski areas in Canada. The Comox Glacier seems close enough to touch from the top of the chair, which runs all summer. "Fun, quality and affordability" is Forbidden's philosophy. The place is known for its friendly atmosphere. Ski theft is virtually unknown. The mountain has a no-nonsense approach to safety on the hill. A family oriented hill, Forbidden keeps costs down for children. A Youth Rate further encourages young people to ski.

Skiing Terrain: 351 m vertical, 40% Novice, 50% Intermediate, 10% Expert. Slopes and trails: Beginner (3), Novice (7), Intermediate (8), and Expert (3). "Jay Way" at 2.4 km is the longest run on Vancouver Island.

Lifts operate 5 days a week, Thursday through Monday (9 to 4) and all school holidays except Christmas Day. CSIA Ski school plus a Kinderski Program including snow "fun" as well as skiing.

Day Lodge & Bar: View of mountains and skiers from both the lounge and cafeteria as well as a fantastic panorama of Comox Valley, the Strait of Georgia and the Canada mainland. Lockers and change rooms. Ski rentals & service (including crosscountry) in adjacent shop.

Crosscountry Skiing: Free beginners loop at the bottom of the hill. A single-track trail leads 5 km from the top of the chair, for advanced intermediate crosscountry skiers. Telemark lessons are available and require advance booking.

Special Events at Mt. Washington & Forbidden

Nov   Ski Fairs & Swaps.
            Warren Miller Movies
Nov-Dec   Grand Opening at Forbidden and Mt.
            Washington
Dec   Wedel Weekend--Early season fun/conditioner
            for all
            Nordic Lessons
            Special Christmas & New Year's Events
            and Parties
Jan   Winter Carnivals & Parades
            Skiing Is Believing Program
            Moonlight Ski
            Para-Ski Meet--Canada's national paraski
            team and U.S. competitors land with para-
            chutes in front of the day lodge, ride the lift
            and ski 2 giant slalom runs.
            Demo Ski Weekend
Feb   Races including Kinder-Ski Race
            Valentine Dance

Ski Comox Valley. (Tourism Comox Valley).

Mar	Forbidden Kandahar Downhill-- Unique race for top notch amateurs from all over Western Canada. Skiers have clocked over 80 mph. Mt. Washington Cross-Country Marathon
Apr	Fun slalom racing
May	Comox Valley Snow-To Surf Race--Wacky parades and race from top of Mt. Washington, over a cross-country course, 2 running legs, bicycling, then canoeing to finish in Comox.

Travel & Lodging

Through Courtenay from the south, the turnoff for skiing is at Condensory Road, just before the Fifth Street bridge. From there, signs clearly indicate which way to go. From the north, new signs direct drivers to the turnoff near Merville, where back roads take you to the hills. Mild weather means easy driving most of the time. You must carry chains to Mt. Washington, 33 km, not required for Forbidden, 22 km.

VIA Rail has a train leaving Victoria every morning at 8:15 am, arriving in Courtenay at 12:45 pm. Buses go up and down the Island and connect to the lower Mainland. Buses are also available south from Port Hardy daily. Ski buses stop at various locations around the Comox Valley and travel to both resorts, arriving in time for a full day of skiing.

Three airlines fly daily to the Comox Valley. Air BC and Time Air run direct flights from Vancouver, flying to Comox airport where taxi service can get you into Courtenay in less than 15 minutes. Car rentals are also available. Burrard Air lands at the Courtenay Air Park, near downtown, also with daily flights from Vancouver.

The Courtenay area offers many excellent hotels, motels and camping.

Mogul Home Park: RV drivers, stay on the hill in comfort at Mt. Washington's 100-site park. Rates are daily (several dollars more with electrical hookup), weekly, monthly or by the season. A recreational center offers lockers, showers, washrooms, a laundromat, games room, sauna and a meeting room. Park guests can reach their RV's by skiing down a trail off the Linton's Loop run.

More information and snow, ski condition reports: Tourism Comox Valley, 830-T Cliffe Ave., Courtenay, B.C. V9N 2J7, (604) 338-1424.

Mount Cain

Travelers and South Islanders are "discovering" the North Island's Family Ski Heaven. Located 12 km off Highway 19,

Ski Comox Valley. (Tourism Comox Valley).

127

halfway between Port Hardy and Campbell River, this area has stunning views in all directions and immediate appeal to skiers getting out in the mountains to escape the glitz of big city life on the mainland.

The Mountain: A recently built T-bar doubled Mount Cain's vertical distance to 394 m, opening up more Advanced and Intermediate terrain on the upper slopes of the 1794 m mountain. Crosscountry skiers enjoy 20 km of unmarked crosscountry trails, including some large open bowls for telemarking. Base elevation is only 1225 m with a long season of fine, deep snow.

Services: Mount Cain opens as soon as snow falls, usually the end of November. The ski shop has a full range of skiing accessories and rental equipment. Qualified instructors teach private and group lessons. There is a snack bar and day lodge. Lift tickets - full and half day - are low, season passes and special group ski rates. Children under 5 and seniors 65 and over ski free! Mount Cain is open 9:30 am to 3:30 pm weekends and holidays.

Travel & Lodging

From Port Hardy, take Hwy 19 south for 124 km, and, 12 km past Woss, turn right (south) on the road to Schoen Lake. Look for signs directing you to turn left (northeast) toward Mount Cain Alpine Park (about 12 km from the highway). From Campbell River (135 km) or Sayward (84 km) go north to the same intersection and turn left to reach the ski area.

Great accommodations in Port Hardy and Port McNeill nearby.

More information & Mount Cain Snowline: Mount Cain Alpine Park Society, Box 1225, Port McNeill, B.C. V0N 2R0, (604) 956-3792. **Mount Cain SNOWLINE: (604) 956-3744**

Mount Arrowsmith

Step into your hiking boots or ski boots! Winter or summer, Port Alberni's Mount Arrowsmith (1817 m) offers a quick getaway to the highlands. The mountain has superb hiking and climbing in the summer. In winter, the downhill ski area operates from December to mid-May, Saturdays, Sundays and Holidays. There are 2 T-bars and a free rope tow running from 9:30 am to 4:00 pm. Crosscountry skiers enjoy Mount Arrowsmith too. Stop in at the day lodge, cafeteria, and lounge. Located south of Hwy 4, about 15 km west of Parksville, the area offers rental equipment and a ski school. Good accommodations in Parksville or Port Alberni.

More Information & Snow-Ski Reports: Alberni Valley Chamber of Commerce, RR2 Site 215, C-10, Port Alberni, B.C. V9Y 716, (604) 724-6535.

Mt. Washington. (Tourism Comox Valley).

Waterfall Entrance to Main Cave, Upana Caves, with ice deposits. (P. Griffiths)

13. CAVING

Vancouver Island is a surprising treasure box of caves. Over a thousand wait for you to explore them. Some require advanced caving, including boats and dive gear. Some are walk-ins that families with children can enjoy, requiring only sensible footgear, jackets, helmets and lights.

Driving the gravel road from Gold River toward Tahsis, about 17 km west of Gold River, I spot a signed dirt road taking off into a group of trees clustered on a logged mountainside. Ahead of me, a young woman gets out of her car wearing a longsleeved shirt and rock climbing pants despite the bright sunshine of the hot August noon. Karen Griffiths, who has 12 years and several thousand hours experience guiding cave tours and teaching, hands me a helmet with a light. I get out a second flashlight and put on the camera pack. We descend a path beside the stand of trees shielding this cave system that the logging company had to leave untouched. In a few meters we reach the first shallow tame-looking caves.

"Here's a natural fault. The water comes down this way, then makes a 90 degree corner along a natural fault in this rock, some type of granite. From there it turns another corner, goes around a little island producing 2 waterfalls. Water won't dissolve this rock away, but it does dissolve the limestone.

"Cavers weren't the first people to see these caves. People doing the roads, doing survey lines, loggers. The area we will enter was logged around 1970-71. This area we're in now was logged in 1980." A packed trail of wood chips leads down the gully. "The Upana Caves system, named after the river that flows through one of the caves, lies under the TFL (tree farm license) of CIP Inc. British Columbia Forest Service administers the caves in cooperation with CIP Inc. The Gold River caving group, part of the B.C. Speleological Federation, looks after maintenance."

Caving

The best seasons to cave on Vancouver Island are spring or summer, when water levels are predictable. Or midwinter, when the snow load is set and frozen. The riskiest time is late fall, when sudden rains can flood the caves and trap cavers. We go through the 'whale mouth' entrance to see ceiling formations that look like the backbone of a whale -- Moby Dick Room. The day outside is hot and sunny. Each time we enter a new hole in the rock, cool air refreshes us. Thrushes nest inside some cave entrances. We climb down through narrow passageways into total darkness broken only by our headlamps. I am glad for the helmet when I bump my head on the rock.

"Large stalactite and stalagmite formations are in many caves. Some appealing shapes are called 'cave popcorn,' 'coral,' or 'cauliflower.' Copper causes a bit of green staining on the rocks. In another cave we'll see a total igneous wall. In some caves, there are ice stalactites and stalagmites. Caves on Vancouver Island have colorful formations created by various minerals leaching through -- pink, orange, purple. Here is some lovely grey and white marble. We try to protect these rare occurrences to make sure they stay intact.

"The Indians did not break off formations in the caves because that was bad luck. Only the chieftain or the medicine man was allowed to take any. Sometimes West Coast Indians used dry caves as burial chambers. One cave found on the northwest side of the Island had skeletons perfectly preserved in woven cedar boxes and a cache of abalone necklaces and glass beads."

"Now we're moving through a phreatic passageway - created by a full torrent of water passing through. The other type is a vadose passageway --narrow then wide then narrow then widens out again--created by centuries of varying water levels. The phreatic tunnels are impressive, with scalloping on the walls caused by lapping water. In Strathcona Park you have to climb to enter some of the caves at 1500 m to 2000 m elevations."

We see a number of pools that Karen says lead to underground passageways, many of them connected, that can be explored only by experienced divers. Karen's voice echoes in one of the largest rooms we enter that has holes in elevated chambers, evidence of water riding up over different rock strata. She shows me where the underground sequences of the TV series "Huckleberry Finn and His Friends" were filmed at the caves in 1979. The girl who played Becky had to wear a light summer dress and lie freezing on the cold rocks waiting for Tom Sawyer to rescue her while the film crew reshot the scene over and over. To see the Upana Caves near Gold River, contact: SpeleoLecTours, Karen Griffiths, Box 897, Gold River, B.C. V0P 1G0, (604)283-2691

A late summer evening in Port Hardy. Mike and Linda Hancock are sharing their living room for a meeting with a muscular mountain guide who looks as if he would feel at home anywhere on the North Island outside 4 walls. In fact, Mike Henwood tells us that when he leaves here he will do a night hike to the base of a peak that he will climb with friends tomorrow.

Henwood is an avid caver. He has climbed extensively with Paul Griffiths, Karen's husband, who is one of Canada's top cavers. Together they have mapped or are planning to map many Vancouver Island caves, an arduous process that requires engineering skills in addition to caving sport proficiency. Mike Henwood runs Mountain Line Tours, a guide service operating out of Port McNeill on the northern end of Vancouver Island. He leads trips that range from 2- hour sightseeing and photography tours to multi-day expeditions down into or high above the earth.

"Depending upon people's experience level, we can put together a package to give them whatever type adventure they want. In order to get into one cave, you rappel over 3 waterfalls - all underground. This is the kind of adventure that we can offer. On the North Island alone we have 1060 caves. Even most people who live here don't know about them.

"We were just camping out in the Atluck Lake area, checking out the Tahsish River drainage, and we ran across caves there in the Canfor claims. The logging company has to stop their operation in this area and clean it up to preserve the cave system. These caves that we found could be made so accessible for the public that it would be phenomenal to do tours there." On a map he points to a 15 km gap between logging roads south of Benson Lake where cavers hope to develop a trail leading to the cave system. "It's going to take us a long time to map it. Paul Griffiths and I have been several hours underground mapping now.

"A cave in Holberg is literally the size of a football stadium. It would be about twice the size of Devil's Bath. Devil's Bath used to be a domed chamber in a limestone cave. The whole thing collapsed and filled up with water. Most likely there was water in it to begin with. Now it's called Devil's Bathtub. Divers have been down 70 m in the Devil's Bathtub and have never come to a bottom. We will be getting submersible video equipment with electronic eyes to see how deep it is. We tried depth sounders and the signal just bounces off the walls. There are sections under the Bath like a big tonsil sticking out. From that lake, there's an underwater passage that goes to the Benson River cave system and many other links beyond that are unexplored. Equally amazing are the Vanishing River, Glory Hole, Eternal Fountain -- such a big cave system, it used to be known as the third deepest cave in Canada. It ends in a sump. You go over 3 stages of 32 m drops. Then you come to water again.

"The B.C. Speleological Federation doesn't open all known caves to the public. They are so spectacular, we're trying to protect them. The risk of vandalism that has happened in some caves is extreme.

"We supply all needed caving equipment, including safety equipment. The majority of serious cavers bring their own equipment--ropes, ascenders, and so on. If we do canoe runs underground, we supply all the equipment. The only thing the customer needs is a sturdy pair of hiking or rock boots or, preferred, runners. We can do the majority of caves here in runners. Where we're climbing and getting in a lot of mud, runners are the best. Unless it's wet, limestone is seldom slippery.

"Island cave systems are generally cool or cold -- averaging 7º C (45ºF). Cavers should have something hot to drink every 3 hours or so. Backup light systems are important. When you shut your light off underground, it's not like shutting a light off in your house. I'm talking complete, absolute blackness. We always go in fully prepared, with 4 sources of light per person.

"Here are photographs of stalactites (icicle-shaped deposits of calcium carbonate hanging from the ceiling) and stalagmites (similar deposits built up from the floor). See how some meet to form a column. People ask about cave-ins: are these caves safe to go into? Well, these delicate formations predate the ice age. These columns, older than 20,000 years, give you a pretty good idea of the stability of these caves.

"People need to understand not to touch any formations inside a cave. In one second you can destroy thousands of years

Caver inspecting calcite column and stalagmite in Mystery Cave, Northern Vancouver Island. (P. Griffiths)

of geological development. It's very tempting when you enter a room and your lights hit a blaze of colors or shining crystals. Without thinking, you naturally reach out. A touch with your fingertip can dislodge fragile pieces or deposit oils and acids that can alter the formation.

"At the end of this passage is a room that is possibly the most decorated cave in Canada. Here is a flowstone formation exactly like what you find in China. Here is Sodastraw Passage, with about a 10 m ceiling, 1.5 m long needle-shaped structures hanging in tight array. The formations are called sodastraws because they have a hole right through the middle of them. Fragile. Breathing on them can break them. Phosphorescence in some rooms looks like silver on the walls. One formation looks like a candlestick sticking out of the wall of a passage.

"We have many options for the "average" trekker or hiker who isn't superman but who enjoys being in the backcountry. One 6-hour tour involves 4 natural phenomena. You enter underground on one leg for a short distance, about 20 m to a lake, and as soon as you shine your lights on it, salmon will appear. Last summer in August we had the salmon there. They were jumping at our feet. They were trapped in the caves. They come in at high water into the bath through the river passage, then.they get stuck when the river drops off. Vancouver Island runoff is so quick and so much. People who have taken this tour were totally impressed by the safari they were on.

"Even locals don't realize what the country really looks like off the main highway. To see the intense beauty of this island, you have to get away from the clearcuts and roadways. Other tour options include stopping at lakes if you want to picnic, floating rivers, or climbing mountains. We have spent years exploring this country, but we're still finding new caves all the time." Contact: Mountain Line Tours, Mike Henwood, P.O. Box 431, Port McNeill, B.C. V0N 2R0, (604) 956-4827.

Bill Shephard, head planner for the Regional District of Mount Waddington, told of the amazing Eternal Fountain, Devil's Bath and Vanishing River Cave trio that the District promotes as a self-guiding adventure. They are within 30 km of Port McNeill just off logging roads. While the District Office is very friendly and helpful about area maps, it is still easy to get lost. On our tour, most of the signs the District put up were gone or knocked over. Either be prepared to be a little lost or arrange for a guide through Mountain Line Tours or SpeleoLecTours. For maps and current logging information, contact: Regional District of Mount Waddington, Box 729, Port McNeill, B.C. V0N 2R0, (604) 956-3301.

Another cave system you can visit farther down-Island is Horne Lake Caves west of Horne Lake. Driving 60 km north from Nanaimo on Hwy 19, turn left at the Horne Lake Cafe, follow the signs 14 km to Horne Lake Campsite then go past the Campsite to Horne Lakes Provincial Park. According to the cave brochure: Horne Lake Main and Lower Main Caves were first reported in 1912 by a local geologist... Several years later, local loggers used the stream issuing from one of the caves to run their steam donkeys. In the spring of 1939, the caves were "rediscovered" by 2 local amateur explorers. Riverbend Cave was discovered and explored more recently. It was subsequently gated to protect it...a display of beautiful crystalline calcite formations. In February 1971, the Horne Lakes Cave Provincial Park was established to protect the caves from any further damage.

These cave guiding services are provided jointly by the Canadian Cave Conservancy and the Vancouver Island Cave Exploration Group under a park use permit issued by the Ministry of Environment and Parks. The tours are not recommended for very young children, people with health problems, or the very elderly. For 1-4 hour tours beginning late spring, contact: Canadian Cave Conservancy, 3841 Hobbs Street, Victoria, B.C. V8N 4C5, (604)757-8541 or Horne Lake Cave Guiding Services, 182 Kenuir Road, Qualicum, B.C.

For information on sport caving, contact knowledgeable and experienced cavers through: British Columbia Speleological Federation, P.O. Box 733, Gold River, B.C. V0P 1G0, (604) 283-2691.

Diver with basketstars

14. DIVING

"Vancouver Island: Cold-water Paradise for Divers"
by Neil McDaniel (all photos by the author)

'Second only to the Red Sea.' That bold statement was made by a well-known National Geographic photographer after his experiences in one of British Columbia's most spectacular underwater regions near the northern tip of Vancouver Island. It is a very complimentary comparison to be sure, but it's likely that many divers have misunderstood what he meant. The Red Sea has warm, blue water. Around Vancouver Island it's cold and green. In the Red Sea underwater visibility exceeds 100 feet; 30 to 40 feet is considered good in Vancouver Island waters. So far the comparison doesn't make much sehse. But when you consider the abundance, diversity and colour of the marine life in these two distinct dive areas, there is a remarkable likeness.

The Red Sea is famous for its gorgonian corals and delicate soft corals. Surprisingly, the plankton-rich, cold waters around Vancouver Island also have an abundance of soft corals and other colourful marine life, due to strong tidal currents that flow through the narrow channels along the coast, carrying suspended food to incredible numbers of sea creatures.

Not all of the Vancouver Island coast is blessed with such abundance, and the best regions are often the remotest ones. The wide range of habitats is largely responsible for the outstanding variety of Vancouver Island diving. Open coast surge-swept shores, steep fjord walls, rocky current-swept channels and quiet protected bays--all harbour their own assembly of plants and animals.

The invertebrates are among the most intriguing animals in Vancouver Island waters, with nearly 30 species of seastars in shallow water, nudibranchs by the dozen, graceful anemones up to 3 feet tall, enormous sea whips over 7 feet high, and giant Pacific octopi that tip the scales at over 100 pounds. While the

139

fish generally lack the bizarre patterns and colours of their tropical counterparts, there are notable exceptions, such as the Red Irish Lord sculpin, decorated warbonnet and several dozen species of strikingly marked rockfish. Large marine mammals are also found, especially the northern sea lions, which can exceed a thousand pounds.

Diving around Vancouver Island is for the adventurous, those who have a bit of the explorer spirit in them--there are literally hundreds of miles of Vancouver Island's 3700 mile long coastline that have never been seen beneath the waves.

Because of coastal British Columbia's mild winters, diving is enjoyed year-round. Plankton levels and freshwater runoff are at their lowest during the winter months, resulting in surprisingly clear water. In some of the best areas underwater visibility can reach almost 80 feet, providing excellent conditions for photography. During spring and summer, plankton blooms and runoff combine to make underwater clarity unpredictable. Often only the surface layer is turbid, with clear water deeper, but this varies..

A good wetsuit or drysuit is a necessity for diving comfortably in Vancouver Island waters, summer or winter. Water temperatures are lowest in late winter, about 41º to 48º F at most depths. In the summer, the surface layer warms considerably (up to 60º F), but below that temperatures stay at 50º F or less, requiring a complete suit with hood, boots and gloves.

Recreational diving is extremely popular in British Columbia and there is a well developed industry with many dive shops, diving resorts, charter boat operations and suit manufacturers. Virtually anything a traveling diver might require, from an 0-ring to repairs on a sophisticated camera, can be found.

Victoria
Victoria is on the southern Vancouver Island at the east end of the Strait of Juan de Fuca, the broad channel that connects the sheltered waters of the Strait of Georgia to the open Pacific Ocean. Tidal currents flowing past Victoria are quite swift,

Sea anemone

resulting in rich marine life. Several excellent shore dive sites are near Victoria, including Saxe Point Park, the Ogden Point Breakwater and Ten-mile Point.

The highlight of this region is unquestionably Race Rocks, 11 miles southwest of Victoria. Topped by a massive black and white stone lighthouse, this cluster of reefs offers some of the most exciting diving on the B.C. coast. Strong currents sweep between the rocks, providing food for a lush growth of invertebrates. One can also expect to see northern sea lions, harbour seals, male California sea lions and even the occasional sea elephant lounging on the low-lying islets.

Below the surface the bottom is thick with colourful life: purple and red hydrocorals; ghostly white plumose anemones; purple, green, orange and red brooding anemones and graceful basketstars extending their many-branched arms into the current flow.

There are several professional dive stores in Victoria, providing full sales, service, rentals and instruction. Many also offer guided charter services. Several resorts offer all-inclusive diving packages for visitors.

Sidney

Sidney is a small community on the eastern shore of Saanich Peninsula facing Haro Strait. Nearby are many islands where there are dive sites, most affected by currents flowing through the Strait. The broken rock sea floor is brightened by gardens of brilliant orange sea cucumbers and a rich variety of colourful nudibranchs which feed on feathery hydroids. In the shallows, pinto abalone are abundant, leaving narrow tracks behind as they scrape algae from the rocks.

In the crook of Saanich Peninsula is Saanich Inlet, a sheltered area that offers an excellent alternative when sea conditions on the 'out-side' are too rough. The inlet has cloud sponge formations below 80 feet, and the water clarity is often exceptional in the winter.

The southern Gulf Islands, including Saltspring, Mayne, North and South Pender and Galiano, can be reached by ferry or charter boat from Sidney and Vancouver and also have resorts that offer accom-modations and compressed air for filling scuba tanks.

Nanaimo

Nanaimo is the end of one of the 2 main ferry routes from mainland British Columbia to Vancouver Island. Only an hour and 45 minutes from Vancouver, Nanaimo is near the northern Gulf Islands where there are several excellent dive sites in current-swept passages such as Dodd Narrows, Gabriola

Passage and Porlier Pass. North of Nanaimo are islands stretching parallel to Vancouver Island which provide charter boat diving areas.

Courtenay

Two large islands off eastern Vancouver Island just south of Courtenay, Denman and Hornby Islands are popular with divers. Hornby, especially, is gaining fame as the home of 6-gill sharks often seen at the southeast corner of the island. Several wrecks here include the *Alpha*, which ran aground on Chrome Island at the southern tip of Denman. There are resorts and several government parks, reached by charter boats operating out of Vancouver and Nanaimo.

Campbell River

Campbell River is at the north end of the Strait of Georgia at the entrance of Discovery Passage. With a superb view across the swirling waters of the passage toward Quadra Island, Campbell River has long been a salmon fisherman's mecca, especially for those chasing the elusive tyee. You can snorkel or scuba dive and watch the salmon underwater.

The excellent diving is popular, and groups dive on the incredibly colourful reefs of Steep Island, Row and Be Damned, Copper Cliffs and Whiskey Point--just a few of the current-swept sites reached by guided charter boats or private boats. Carpeted with strawberry anemones and encrusting sponges of nearly every colour of the rainbow, the reefs of Discovery Passage rival any in beauty.

As a salmon fishing centre, Campbell River has hotels, motels and resorts offering a wide range from deluxe to rustic accommodations. Special diving packages are available which include meals, accom-modations, and boat charters with an experienced divemaster.

Port McNeill

At the northern end of Johnstone Strait lies the fishing and logging town of Port McNeill, close to some excellent diving areas. This region has strong currents and marine life similar to that of Race Rocks, with pink coral-like branching hydrocorals, blankets of rose soft corals, plumose anemones and countless basketstars. During the spring and summer lush forests of kelp ring most of the reefs and islets, providing intriguing backgrounds for underwater photography. This area is an important passage for orcas (killer whales) from Queen Charlotte Strait into Johnstone Strait and diver sightings are frequent in summer when the whales spend much of their time around Robson Bight, just south of Port McNeill.

Port Hardy

Near the northern end of Vancouver Island, Port Hardy provides access to the many reefs of Queen Charlotte Strait, an area just be-ginning to be explored. The reefs have a unique blend of current-swept and open coast marine life outstanding in variety and abundance. Mild to strong currents flow through passages between the tightly-grouped islands, supporting soft corals, anemones, sponges and forest-like groves of kelp .

Accommodations and charter boats are available in Port Hardy. Several Vancouver-based charter operators are stationed in Port Hardy during summer.

Ucluelet

Barkley Sound is the southernmost inlet on the west coast of the Island, a scenic area including part of Canada's Pacific Rim Park, the Broken Islands. The richest zone of marine life is in the shallows, most often at depths less than 30 feet. Here swells from the open Pacific surge around hundreds of reefs which pierce the surface of the Sound. The marine life is diverse and quite different from that in sheltered waters such as the Strait of Georgia. Massive colonies of branching bryozoans create coral-like reefs which provide shelter for brittle stars, juvenile crabs and brilliantly marked ring-top snails. On sloping drop-offs in sheltered deeper water are large populations of feather-stars, trapping food with their foot long plume-like rays.

Barkley Sound is famous for its dazzling variety of rockfish. On steeper walls divers find blue, black, widow and canary rockfish schooling off the bottom, while china, vermilion, quillback, tiger, yelloweye and Puget Sound rockfish cruise closer to the sea floor. The grey, wizened heads of wolf-eels poke from countless caves and crannies.

Accommodations are plentiful at Ucluelet, Port Alberni, and Bamfield, and compressed air and boat charters are available.

Neil Glenn McDaniel: Certified as a scuba diver in 1969, Neil McDaniel has made the underwater world an important part of his life since his graduation from the Marine Zoology program at the University of British Columbia. For 7 years he was an ecological technician with Fisheries and Oceans Canada, studying intertidal, shallow-water and deep habitats along the length of Canada's west coast. A widely published writer and photographer, he became editor of Diver Magazine in 1981 and continues to dive avidly, specializing in still, video and underwater filming.

Dive shops have equipment and services in Campbell River, Courtenay, Duncan, Gabriola Island, Galiano Island, Ganges, Nanaimo, Port Alberni, Port Hardy, Sidney, Ucuelet, Victoria. Obtain Tide Tables and Canadian Nautical Charts from the Canadian Hydrographic Service (Ch 19, Maps).

For more Vancouver Island diving information, read: *141 Dives in the Protected Waters of Washington and British Columbia* by Betty Pratt-Johnson, Gordon Soules Publisher C302-355 Burrard St, Vancouver, B.C. V6C 2G6, (604) 688-5466 and

Diver Magazine(USA) PO Box 984, Point Roberts, WA 98281.(Canada) P.O. Box 1312, Delta, B.C. V4M 3Y8, (604) 273-4333

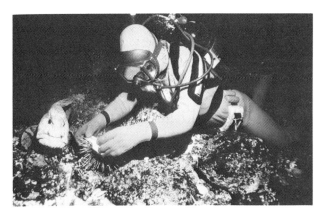

Diver feeds wolf-eel at Egmont, B.C.

Friday Harbor, San Juan Islands, from ferry to Sidney, B.C.

15. GULF ISLANDS

Discovery, the essence of legends in the Northwest, takes form in the Gulf Islands. Aesthetic discovery is the prime mover of the islands' economy today. Freelance artists live and work on more than 100 islands in the Strait of Georgia. With their surprisingly high hills and irregular shorelines, these Canadian islands are similar to the U.S. San Juans to the south. The weather here is the best in Canada--Mediterranean temperatures and sunshine with protected waters for divers, sailors, and fishermen. The Gulf Islands lie east of Vancouver Island between the latitudes of Nanaimo and the Saanich Peninsula just north of Victoria.

Travelers to the Gulf Islands today follow discovery begun by navigator Juan de Fuca in 1592 and continued by Spanish and English explorers. Sailing through the Islands for the first time, these Euro-peans left their mark in names on the charts they made to guide succeeding visitors. Saturna Island was named for the Spanish naval schooner *Saturna* that arrived in the 1790's. Pender Island's name comes from Captain Daniel Pender, who surveyed this water in the 1860's. Galiano Island was named for Dionysio Galiano, commander of the Spanish squadron sent to explore the Pacific Northwest in the 1790's. Natives considered Salt Spring Island the enclave of a deity. It was a site for feasts and funerals, but not for permanent living.

From the West Coast (Nootka), Kwakiutl and Coast Salish to the Haida, Indians with a distinct culture were Gulf Island natives thousands of years before foreign visitors brought alcohol, machinery, their own dogma, and diseases. Permanent settlers arrived in the 1850's, led by a group of ex-slaves from the American South who landed at Vesuvius Bay on Salt Spring in 1857. Two years later, when expeditions discovered gold on the Fraser River on mainland Canada, people settled on Mayne Island and spread to bays and inlets through-out the Gulf Islands.

147

The new island residents depended on agriculture. By the1900's, Salt Spring had 80 farms and was noted for producing butter. Meanwhile, Mayne Island became known for orchards and is said to be the first place in British Columbia where apple trees grew.

Fishing was important during the region's early days. Salteries and fish plants sprang up on the islands. The original pilings of some salteries are still visible on the west coast of Galiano Island. Today, a small fleet of fishing boats calls the Gulf Islands home, but they do most of their fishing in distant waters.

The lumber industry has survived on the Gulf Islands. Many plants operate log booming, small-scale milling and logging operations. MacMillan-Bloedel, for example, owns much of Galiano Island, and the company maintains a camp there.

Tourism as been a Gulf Islands industry since the late 1800's, when Mayne Island had 2 hotels at Miner's Bay. Resorts were built in the 1900's, starting a tradition of catering to visitors that continues today.

Today, hundreds of retirees live in the islands, attracted by the peace and quiet of local life as well as the climate. This is an important center for artists--painters, photographers, writers, musicians--many of international reputation, who live, work and teach here. Craftsmen pursue cottage industries designing and making instruments, boatbuilding, potting, carving, weaving, and producing other fine crafts. With the rising population, real estate costs and taxes have risen dramatically.

The growth of government in these islands has not followed the growth of population. There are no incorporated cities or municipalities (Ganges incorporated briefly in the 1880's, but the Province rescinded the order after disagreements occurred), and the regional districts have limited authority. The Islands Trust--an organization with 2 representatives from each of 13 islands in the Strait of Georgia--functions as the local government. Established by the B.C. Legislature in the 1970's, the Trust plans and directs land use. In 1975, the Islands Trust teamed with the Nature Conservancy of Canada to produce an inventory of natural areas in the Gulf Islands and make recommendations on their conservation. Under one section, entitled "Need for Preservation in the Islands Trust Area," the report says: "The Islands Trust area, as part of the Strait of Georgia-Puget Sound region, can readily be considered the most important area for outdoor recreation in North America. Few other areas of the world offer such a diversity of reacreational and aesthestic values. In addition, the area's dry, mild climate, outstanding marine resources and unique flora and fauna make it one of the most interesting environmental regions in Canada."

These beautiful islands, from expansive bodies of land with farms and small mountains on them to a few meters of rock jutting from Strait waters, are so complex that they can only be described properly in a full-length book. In fact, Bruce Obee wrote *The Gulf Islands Explorer* (18. Good Reading). With assistance from the Tourism Association of Vancouver Island and Travel Infocentres, I am giving you current data to start your own exploration, using either the Continent or Vancouver Island as a takeoff point.

Like other desirable travel destinations in the world, the Gulf Islands are fragile, and you need to share responsibility for preserving them whenever you visit. Wildland and building fires are a problem. Most visitors do not realize that many of these islands, surrounded by water, do not have natural sources of fresh water. If a fire starts high on one of their steep cliffs or across broad fields, there is no easy way to put it out. Fire suppression by air (fixed wing and helicopters) is incredibly expensive and limited in scope. Ground fire crews take time to arrive and require setting up a complete headquarters(feeding, sleeping, supply, etc.). Despite everything that can be done, especially in the dry late summer, fighters cannot always stop a fire. Uncontrolled fires do damage that lasts years, sometimes wiping out whole plant or animal populations. They risk human lives.

Another problem is visitor thoughtlessness--littering, trespassing on private land, rude driving (cars, bicycles, and boats). The beaches are crown (public) land up to the high tide mark, but you need to consult maps and Infocentres to find out where you can holiday without disturbing island residents. Some entire islands are private holdings, where you cannot land without prior permission. Put yourself in islander's shoes. He lives and works here and has to deal with what happens after you leave.

Come to the Gulf Islands prepared for what you want to do. If you will be canoeing, kayaking, sailing, or traveling by powerboat, get the charts and tide tables you need from the Canadian Hydrographic Service (19. Maps). These include the *Canadian Tide & Current Tables*, Vol. 5, titled "Juan de Fuca and Georgia Straits," the *Small Craft Guide*, and set No. 3310 of 4 charts: *Gulf Islands--Victoria Harbour to Nanaimo Harbour*. Several local newspapers and AM radio stations broadcast daily tides and weather information. Obviously, you will need a compass, possibly all your own fresh water, and appropriate safety-survival gear. Only expert paddlers should challenge the extreme hazards of waters through Active Pass or Porlier Pass. If you will be hiking or bicycling, get topographic and road maps for the right islands and come equipped for bad weather, breakdowns, and emergency field medicine. The islands are popular, even beyond the summer-fall season. Regardless of your transportation, if you hope to stay in hotels, campsites or other accommodations here, **make reservations well in advance**.

The advantage of traveling without a car on the ferry is that you can take a kayak, canoe, or bicycle along as baggage. Before every trip, whether on foot, driving your car or bringing an RV, **check current ferry schedules and regulations** (B.C. or U.S., as appropriate). Some require advance reservations.

Marine Harbours & Parks

Boating in the waters of the Gulf Islands offers visitors a chance to follow the wake of the early explorers, as well as a visit to out-of-the-way coves and scenes the land-locked traveler misses. Throughout the islands, 16 harbours offer refuge with amenities for sailors. The harbours are run by

Transport Canada or the Department of Fisheries and Oceans, through its Small Craft Harbours branch. The *Guide to Federal Fishing and Recreational Harbours: British Columbia* published by the Canadian government contains a complete list of harbours and services. All west coast B.C. geography is covered. You can get copies in most harbour facilities. Five provincial marine parks on South Pender, Saturna, Galiano, and Portland Islands cater to visitors.

Follow the map for an imaginary sailing rundown of the harbours offering shelter in the Gulf Islands:

At Galiano, the sailor can go around the island and never be far from a haven. At the south end of Active Pass, Sturdies Bay contains 48 m of berth space and a derrick for boat repairs. The bay sits close to the commercial center of the island. Rounding Gossip Island and moving into the Strait of Georgia brings the sailor to Whaler Bay, which offers 185 m of wharf space and a chance to dispose of garbage. Cruising up the Strait, the sailor reaches the island's north end, where the North Galiano wharf contains berthage space. You can then swing down Trincomali Channel to Retreat Cove, which provides 49 m of berthage space.

Further south is Montague Harbour, another commercial center on Galiano. At that haven, tucked in behind Parker Island, the berthage space extends for 103 m. Montague Harbour marine park on the southwest shore was the first marine park established in British Columbia, in 1959. Covering 239 acres, it provides a wharf, 25 mooring buoys, boat ramp, 27-unit campground for boaters and tenters, and 30 sites for campers in vehicles. During an archaeological dig in 1964-5, more than 1000 stone and bone artifacts were unearthed from the shell beaches surrounding the park. Trails lead through the nearby coastal forest. The upland has stands of broadleaf maple, Douglas fir, red cedar, giant fir, hemlock, alder, arbutus, oregon grape, salal, wild rose and marsh grass. There is also a saltwater marsh in the park, with a variety of unusual marine life. The owners of the Hummingbird Inn, a pub on Galiano, operate a shuttle bus from the park gates to their doors.

A trip through Active Pass, separating Galiano and Mayne Islands, brings the sailor to Miner's Bay, close to the commercial center of Mayne and provides 47 m of wharf and berthage space.

At Pender Island, the sailor can begin at Port Washington on Swanson Channel. Port Wash, as locals call it, has 112 m of docking space and a slip for launching boats. The port also has an aircraft float.

Continuing around the south end of North Pender Island, you come into Bedwell Harbour. Beaumont Provincial Marine Park is on the northeastern shore of Bedwell Harbour with 15 mooring buoys, picnic tables and campsites. Near Bedwell Harbour Resort, where Canadian Customs clears about 12,000 American boaters each year, the park covers 146 acres and offers undeveloped beaches, pleasant wooded walking trails and a path up Mount Norman, at 270 m the highest point on South Pender. The marine park has been "adopted" by the Pender Island Yacht Club, meaning representatives are on hand to provide information about the area to visiting boaters. Bedwell Harbour Resort has boater services, a waterfront restaurant, solar-heated swimming pool, showers, and laundry facilities.

A short distance north and through the canal separating North and South Pender, the sailor reaches Browning Harbour and a wharf containing 50 m of berth space.

From Browning Harbour, head for Saturna Island and the facilities at Lyall Harbour. The harbour is close to a small commercial wharf and contains 124 m of wharf and berth space. This most remote of the Gulf Islands has 2 provincial marine parks--Cabbage Island Marine Park, located 4 km west of East Point, and Winter Cove marine park at the northwestern end of Saturna. Cabbage is a 10 acre island with a broad, sandy beach for sunbathing plus nearby reefs and inlets to explore by kayak or dinghy. A trail runs around the island and through its forests of arbutus, Douglas fir, cedar and alder. The park offers 15 mooring buoys and toilet facilities.

Winter Cove marine park covers 223 acres and provides secure and sheltered anchorage. Strong tidal currents push through Boat Passage, exciting whitewater for kayakers. Onshore, an easy trail goes through the forest and along the shoreline with places to stop and enjoy the views. The park is also accessible by road. Area residents have built a baseball diamond for visitors' use, and nearby are a grass picnic area, pit toilets, water and information shelters. Note: Winter Cove is one of the few marine parks in B.C. where onshore camping is **not** permitted.

Leaving Saturna, the sailor navigates Plumper Sound to Haro Strait and runs across Swanson Channel to Fulford Harbour on Salt Spring. At the head of the bay, a small commercial center awaits. The harbour offers 73m of space at one wharf, where you can dispose of garbage and get fresh water, and 12m of space at a second wharf.

Racing Tubs come in all shapes. (Tourism Nanaimo)

South of Ruckle Park on Salt Spring Island, Portland Island is home to Princess Margaret Marine Park. Except for water and toilets, the island is undeveloped. People have tried, though. The island's first outside visitors were the Kanakas, Hawaiians brought to Canada by the Hudson's Bay Company. In the late 1800's, Hawaiian-style luaus made the island famous. Other owners have included turn-of-the-century author, poet and Imperialist Sir Clive Phillips-Woolley. In the 1920's, General Frank "One Arm" Sutton owned it. He was an adventurer who once served as a general for Chinese warlords and who later died in a prisoner-of-war camp in World War II. Over the years Portland has been logged and farmed, but nature is slowly reclaiming the land. Today trails lead through old orchards and forests of arbutus, fir, aspen and wild rose. Best anchorages are behind Chad Island and at Tortoise Bay. The Royal Victoria Yacht Club has adopted the park.

The sailor can now set a course for Satellite Channel, running across the south end of Salt Spring and swinging up to Musgrave Landing. The cove is isolated but offers up to 30 m of wharf and berth space. Continuing up Sansum Narrows, there is Burgoyne Bay on the starboard side. Burgoyne shelters a log-sorting operation, so exercise caution. The wharf has 21 m of space. Further north on Stuart Channel is Vesuvius Bay. The ferry from Vancouver Island stops here, and the wharf has 29 m berthage.

The trip continues up Stuart Channel through Houston Passage and on to Trincomali Channel. South of the passage, Fernwood dock has 24 m of space. Cruising southbound down Trincomali Channel, the sailor hits Captain Passage between Salt Spring and Prevost Islands. That waterway leads to Ganges Harbour, the main commercial center for the Gulf Islands, offering 3 government wharves for moorage. A breakwater protects the boat basin which contains 653 m of boat space. The wharf is also home to the Salt Spring fishing fleet. On the other arm of the harbor, there are 2 government wharves: 1 for the Coast Guard only, 1 for transient vessels only.

Although the harbours are government-run, you will find space at a premium.

Salt Spring Island

Size: 180 sq km

Population: 5450 (1981 census)

Towns: Ganges (liquor, fuel, post office, food), Fernwood, Fulford, Vesuvius

Accommodations: Ch 17.

Campsites: Ruckle Park at Beaver Point & Mouat's Provincial Park at Ganges

Saltspring is the largest Gulf Island and has the earliest records of settlement. Called Klaathem (salt) by native Indians, the island is 29 km long and from 11-16 km wide. There are about

160 km of road, mostly paved. Mouat Provincial Park, on the outskirts of Ganges, has 15 campsites and 6 picnic tables. Ruckle Provincial Park, in the southeast corner of Saltspring, has 10 campsites and picnic tables. Mt. Bruce (700 m) is the highest on the island, offering a 360º view, accessible by jeep or truck. Mt. Maxwell (585 m) has views of Samson Narrows and Fulford Valley. From Mt. Tuam, you can see south and west.

Historical buildings are an old 1-room school on Beaver Point Road and 3 old churches at Fulford and North End Road. There are 4 lakes are suitable for public swimming and 4 tennis courts. Saltspring has a full range of retail, commercial, professional, and trade services. Many artists, entertainers and craftsmen have made the island their home, including wildlife painter Robert Bateman and poet Phyllis Webb. Several art galleries, concerts, and crafts fairs have made Saltspring widely known in the art world.

How to get here: B.C. Ferries from Swartz Bay or Crofton on Vancouver Island & Tsawwassen on the mainland. See current B.C. Ferries Schedule. Also Harbour Air Service, Saltspring Island Taxi.

Celebrations: Jun--Flower Shows, Sea Capers, Annual Art Show

Aug --Jazz Festival, Sailing Regatta

Sep--Farmers Market

Golf: Saltspring Island Golf & Country Club (9 holes)

Boat Launch: Goverment Boat Basin, Ganges

Mayne Island

Size: 21 sq km

Population: 553 (1981 census)

Towns: Miners Bay (liquor, fuel, post office, food), Bennett Bay

Accommodations: Many hotels and B&B's (Ch 17.)

Campsites: None

Mayne Island is covered with reminders of people and events that shaped the island as it is today. Mayne is supposedly the only Gulf Island where Captain Vancouver landed. Miners on their way to the Cariboo Gold Rush stopped over in Miner's

Bay. The hotel they stayed in still stands. Japanese began settling on the island in the early 1900s and planted many acres of tomatoes. B.C. apples first grew here. Still standing is a tiny Gaol (jail) built in 1894 for detention of the unruly. You can see St. Mary Magdalene Church, built in 1897. Many galleries have local artwork.

How to get here: B.C. Ferry from Swartz Bay, Vancouver Island and Tsawwassen, mainland. See current B.C. Ferries Schedule.

Celebrations: Summer Maynia Festival
Mayne Island Fall Fair
Labour Day Lion's Salmon Bake
Boat Launch: Potato Point, David Cove, Piggott Bay
Public Beach: Bennett Bay

Gabriola Island

Location: East of Nanaimo
Population: 1630
Accommodations: Ch 17.
Campsites: Private -- Ch 17

At the end of Malaspina Drive, a footpath winds out onto a rocky point where the Malaspina Galleries sit on the edge of the small bay. A ledge forms the floor of the Galleries, while overhead curves a roof of sandstone. East 1 km along Taylor Bay Road is Gabriola Sands Provincial Park, straddling a narrow neck of land between 2 bays and offering protected swimming, sandy beaches and picnicking under the trees. Drumberg Provincial Park at the southern end of Gabriola offers lovely beach walks. Camping is not allowed at either of the provincial parks. There are private campsites and hotel facilities on the island. A store sells supplies. Berry Point, a beach at the northeastern tip of the island, has a great view of the Entrance Island Lighthouse.

How to get here: B.C. Ferries from Nanaimo
Golf: Silva Bay Golf Course

Galiano Island

Size: 57 sq km
Population: 721 (1981 census)

Towns: Sturdies Bay (liquor store, fuel, post office, groceries)
Accommodations: Ch 17.
Campsites: Montague Harbour Park

Halfway between Vancouver and Victoria, Galiano Island is a con-venient stopover of great natural beauty in a quiet, rural atmosphere. The island has several ferries each day coming into Montague Harbour and Sturdies Bay.

Forested in Douglas fir and other west coast trees, the island has thriving arbutus and dogwood. There are oceanfront parks, clamshell beaches, sandstone cliffs, woodland trails, mountain hikes, and abundant wildlife. Rent a boat or charter a catamarran to explore the coastline and fish for salmon or sightsee secluded trails on horseback. Find yourself a sheltered cove and tan on a sizzling summer afternoon as the tide laps in over rocks. Clear waters and spectacular sealife are well known to scuba and skin divers. Relax with a golf game on a 9-hole public course. Visit the cooperative art gallery run by artists. Local inhabitants are self-reliant. Meet some at the pub over a game of darts. On a full moon evening, watch Mt. Baker snows reflect the light 145 km to the southeast.

Places to stay range from log chalets, oceanfront cottages, B&B's to campsites in Montague. Country stores supply provisions or you may dine at several fine restaurants.

How to get here: B.C. Ferries from Swartz Bay, Vancouver Island, and Tsawwassen, mainland. See current B.C. Ferries Schedule.
Celebrations: Jun--Galiano Weavers Exhibit
                  Jul--North Galiano Jamboree, Artists
                  Guild Exhibit
                  Aug--Lion's "Fiesta"
Golf: Galiano Golf & Country Club (9 holes)
Boat Launch: Montague Harbour Marine Park

North & South Pender Islands

Size: 24 sq km
Population: 1020 (1981 census)
Towns: Driftwood Centre (liquor, fuel, post office, food), Port Washington, Magic Lake

157

Accommodations: Lodges, B&B's (Ch 17)
Campsites: Prior Centennial Park, Beaumont Provincial Marine Park

North Pender Island is famous for its hospitality and rural charm. Before the rock isthmus that joined North and South Pender was blasted out and a canal dredged to separate them in 1903, you had to portage boats across. In 1950, a bridge connected the 2 islands, so both are easily toured. Swim and fish either island. Hike up Bald Cone (12 m) and Mount Norman (260 m) for lookout points. South Pender has camping, picnicking sites and drinking water. During summer at Bedwell Harbour, there is a Canadian Customs Port of Entry for air and sea craft. Take a summer tour to a Salish Indian archeology dig on the North Pender Island side of the canal.

How to get here: B.C. Ferries from Swartz Bay, Vancouver Island and Tsawwassen, mainland. See current B.C. Ferries Schedule.
Celebrations: Jun--Library Swap & Shop
Jul--Arts & Crafts Fair
Aug--Fall Fair
Sep--Pender Treck
Golf: North Pender Island Golf & Country Club (9 holes)
Boat Launch: Browning Harbour, Otter Bay
Public Beach: South Pender, just over bridge on left

Saturna Island

Size: 31 sq km
Population: 229 (1981 census)
Towns: Saturna Point (liquor, fuel, pub, food), Boot Cove
Accommodations: Limited (Ch 17)
Campsites: None

Russels Beach on the Gulf side of the island is private property, but they allow swimming and picnicking. Check out the TV transmitter site for great view. Also East Point Lighthouse, about 16 km from dock. A trail climbs to a small barren plateau. The coast is sandstone shaped by the pounding sea. From here you can see the U.S. Coast Guard Station on Patos Island and Mt. Constitution on Orcas Island in the San Juans.

How to get here: B.C. Ferries from Swartz Bay, Vancouver Island and Tsawwassen, mainland. See current B.C. Ferries Schedule.

Celebrations: Jul 1st -- Saturna Island Lamb Barbecue held on private property at Breezy Bay, access via private boat. The event began in 1950, when a handful of local residents gathered to roast a few lambs. Today, as many as 26 lambs are spit roasted, and several thousand visitors line up for dinner. Have fun all day at the old fashioned country fair, craft sale, and beer garden.

Thetis Island

Population: 200
Accommodations: Ch 17.

A small Gulf Island (8 km X 4 km), Thetis is mostly private residences but has Telegraph Harbour Resort, one of the safest and best moorages in the area. Travelers will find a marina and store facilities open in summer. Three summer bible camps are on this island.

How to get here: B.C. Ferries from Chemainus. Check schedules.

The ferry route between Vancouver Mainland (Tsawwassen) and the Gulf Islands is so busy, you have to make vehicle reservations in advance. Have your license number ready when you phone for a reservation.

More Information:

Tourism Association of Vancouver Island or Travel Infocentres on Galiano Island, Saltspring Island, or in Nanaimo (Ch 16. Tourist Information).

Ferry travelers.

16. TOURIST INFORMATION

Here are the courteous, friendly people mentioned throughout this book who will provide extensive information to help you plan trips to Vancouver Island:

Tourism Association of Vancouver Island
302-45 Bastion Square, Victoria, B.C. V8W 1J1   (604)382-3551

Alert Bay Travel Infocentre   (604) 974-5213
Village of Alert Bay   All year
Box 28
Alert Bay, B.C. V0N 1A0

Bamfield Travel Infocentre   (604) 728-3213
Bamfield Chanber of Commerce   Seasonal
Box 5
Bamfield, B.C. V0R 1B0

Campbell River Travel Infocentre   (604) 286-0764
Campbell River & District   All Year
Chamber of Commerce
P.O. Box 400
Campbell River, B.C. V9W 5B6

Chemainus Travel Infocentre   (604) 246-3944
Chemainus & District Chamber of Commerce
P.O. Box 575
Chemainus, B.C. V0R 1K0

Courtenay Travel Infocentre   (604) 334-3234
Comox Valley Chamber of Commerce   All Year
2040 Cliffe Avenue
Courtenay, B.C. V9N 2L3

Cowichan Lake Travel Infocentre   (604) 749-4141
Cowichan Lake District Chamber of Commerce Seasonal
Box 824
Lake Cowichan, B.C. V0R 2G0

Information

Cumberland Travel Infocentre Cumberland Chamber of Commerce Box 74 Cumberland, B.C. V0R 1S0	(604) 336-6261 All Year
Duncan Travel Infocentre Duncan-Cowichan Chamber of Commerce 381 Hwy 1 Duncan, B.C. V9L 3R5	(604) 746-4421 All Year
Galiano Island Travel Infocentre Galiano Island Chamber of Commerce Box 73 Galiano Island, B.C. V0N 1P0	(604) 539-2233 Seasonal
Gold River Travel Infocentre Gold River Chamber of Commerce Box 39 Gold River, B.C. V0P 1G0	(604) 283-2202 Seasonal
Ladysmith Travel Infocentre Ladysmith Chamber of Commerce Box 598 Ladysmith, B.C. V0R 2E0	(604) 245-4846 Seasonal
Nanaimo Travel Infocentre Nanaimo Tourist & Convention Bureau 266 Bryden Street Nanaimo, B.C. V9S 1A8	(604) 754-8474 All year
Parksville Travel Infocentre Parksville & District Chamber of Commerce Box 99 Parksville, B.C. V0R 2S0	604) 248-3613 All year
Port Alberni Travel Infocentre Alberni Valley Camber of Commerce RR#2, Suite 215, C-10 Port Alberni, B.C. V9Y 7L6	(604) 724-6535 All year

Port Hardy Travel Infocentre
Port Hardy & District Chamber of Commerce
Box 249
Port Hardy, B.C. V0N 2P0

(604) 949-7622
All year

Port McNeill Travel Infocentre
Port McNeill & District
Chamber of Commerce
Box 129
Port McNeill, B.C. V0N 2R0

(604) 956-3356
All Year

Port McNeill Travel Infocentre
Regional District of Mt. Waddington
Tourist Advisory Commission
Box 720
Port McNeill, B.C. V0N 2R0

(604) 956-3301
Seasonal

Qualicum Bay Travel Infocentre
Lighthouse Country Business Assoc.
RR#3, Site 351, C-2
Qualicum Bay, B.C. V0R 2T0

(604) 757-9353
Seasonal

Qualicum Beach Travel Infocentre
Qualicum Beach Chamber of Commerce
Box 103
Qualicum Beach, B.C. V0R 2T0

(604) 752-9532
All year

Sidney Travel Infocentre
Saanich Peninsula Tourist Information Centre
Box 2014, 9670 1st Street
Sidney, B.C. V8L 3S3

(604) 656-3616
All year

Saltspring Is. Travel Infocentre
Saltspring Island Tourist Information Centre
Box 111
Ganges, B.C. V0S 1E0

(604) 537-5252

Information

Sooke Travel Infocentre   (604) 642-6112
Sooke-Jordan River Chamber of Commerce   All year
Box 18
Sooke, B.C. V0S 1N0

Tofino Travel Infocentre   (604) 725-3719
Tofino-Long Beach Information Bureau   Seasonal
Box 476
Tofino, B.C. V0R 2Z0

Ucluelet Travel Infocentre   (604) 726-7123
Ucluelet-Port Alberni Tourist   All year
Information Centre
Box 428, #5 - 1620 Peninsula Road
Ucluelet, B.C. V0R 3A0

Victoria Travel Infocentre   (604)382-2127
Tourism Victoria   All year
812 Wharf Street
Victoria, B.C. V8W 1T3

Victoria Travel Infocentre   (604) 478-1130
Juan de Fuca Chamber of Commerce   All year
697 Goldstream Avenue
Victoria, B.C. V9B 2X2

The **Traveler** has been prepared with great attention to accuracy, but since names, addresses and phone numbers can change I am not responsible for errors or omissions in this book.

Emergency

Dial "O" and ask for Royal Canadian Mounted Police (R.C.M.P.) or other emergency service numbers. **Travel Prepared.**

May through September is busy season for travel to Vancouver Island. Holidays and weekends, especially Friday and Sunday afternoons, can be busy any time of year. Since all public access to or from the Island is by ferry or airline, you should make reservations for both travel and accomodations well ahead.

Traveling on the Ferry

Alaska Marine Highway System--P.O. Box R, Juneau, AK 99811

Reservations U.S.: (800) 642-0066. Other: (907) 465-3941

Prince Rupert Terminal: (604) 627-1744

Goes to: Prince Rupert to Skagway. Ports of call: Ketchikan, Wrangell, Petersburg, Sitka, Juneau, Haines. 34-56 hours, 100 cars, 500 passengers. (reservations). The Alaska ferry sailing from Seattle does not stop in Canada, but sails direct to Ketchikan.

Alberni Marine Transportation Co.--Box 188, Port Alberni V9Y 7M7

Reservations: (604) 723-8313

Goes to: Port Alberni to Bamfield & Barkley Sound Points. 9 hours (round trip), 100 passengers, year round, T,Th,S (Su Seasonal). Port Alberni to Ucluelet and Broken Group Islands. 10 hours (round trip), 100 passengers. Seasonal M, W, F.

British Columbia (BC) Ferry Corporation--1112 Fort Street, Victoria V8V 4V2

BC Ferries Information:

(24-hour recorded) Vancouver (604) 685-1021; Victoria (604) 656-0757; Nanaimo (604) 753-6626

(live) Vancouver (604) 669-1211; Victoria (604) 386-3431; Nanaimo (604) 753-1261

Goes to: South Island--Vancouver (Tsawwassen) to Victoria (Swartz Bay), 1 hr 35 min, 300 cars, 1350 passengers; Vancouver (Horseshoe Bay) to Nanaimo (Departure Bay), 1 hr 35 min, 362 cars, 1500 passengers. Gulf Islands (inquire about terminal locations and service); Brentwood (Saanich) to Mill Bay, 20 min, 16 cars, 168 passengers.

North Island--Vancouver Island (Port Hardy) to Prince Rupert, 15 hr day cruise in summer, year round service, weekly call in at Bella Bella, 157 cars (reservations required), 800 passengers. Prince Rupert to Skidegate, year round service, 8 hrs, 80 vehicles (reservations required), 430 passengers; Campbell River (Vancouver Island) to Quathiaski Cove

(Quadra Island), 15min, 30 cars, 200 passengers; Alert Bay Ferry (Cormorant Island), Sointula (Malcolm Island), Port McNeill (Vancouver Island), 30 cars, 150 passengers.

Ferry dock locations--

Tsawwassen: From Vancouver, Hwy 17 South leads to Tsawwassen terminal. From Washington State, Interstate 5 becomes Hwy 99 at Blaine, then follow signs to Hwys 10 & 17. From the east, follow signs on Hwy 1 to Hwys 10 & 17. Tsawwassen is 37 km from downtown Vancouver, a 45 minute drive. Note that in winter, the ferry to Port Hardy and on to Prince Rupert terminates here.

Swartz Bay: 32 km north of Victoria on Hwy 17, about 1/2 hour drive.

Horseshoe Bay: Hwy 1 West leads to Horseshoe Bay. From downtown Vancouver, follow signs through Stanley Park, across the Lion's Gate Bridge to West Vancouver, and along Hwy 99-1 to the ferry terminal, a 21 km drive.

Departure Bay: 3 km north of Nanaimo's city center.

Summer (mid-June to mid-September) sailings are every hour on the hour from 7am to 10pm. Be there 1 hour before sailing. If you are traveling by bicycle, pay at the vehicle booth for your bicycle and yourself. From late May to early September, a scheduled shuttle takes bicycles and their riders through the Deas Island Tunnel (between Vancouver and Tsawwassen Terminal on Hwy 99) during peak traffic periods, call (604) 277-2115 in Vancouver. Pay parking available at the docks is at a premium weekends and holidays. Instead, take a bus to the terminal if you aren't taking your car on the ferry. There are special facilities for the disabled; ask in advance.

Port Hardy: At north end Vancouver Island (driving time--8 hrs from Victoria, 6 hrs from Nanaimo, 3 hrs from Campbell River), the Port Hardy terminal at Bear Cove is 7 km from downtown connected by taxi or minibus.

Prince Rupert on Kaien Island, connected to B. C. mainland, is at western end of Hwy 16, terminal 2 km from town reached by taxi or bus. CP Air, Grayhound Bus & VIA Rail also serve Prince Rupert. From their adjacent dock, the Alaska state ferries sail north to Skagway and the Panhandle. The B.C. ferries north of Port Hardy have besides their surcharge for vehicles over 20' long, another for vehicles over 6'8" high. You may reconsider that cartop carrier if you don't need it.

British Columbia Steamship Company Ltd.--254 Belleville Street, Victoria V8V 1W9

Victoria Reservations: (604) 386-6731; Information: (604) 386-1124

Seattle Reservations: (206) 441-8200; Information (206) 441-5560

Goes to: Daily cruises between Seattle Terminal, Pier 69, 2700 Alaskan Way, and Victoria Terminal, 254 Belleville St.

Ships: *Princess Marguerite*, 50 cars, 1800 passengers, May to October; *Vancouver Island Princess*, 140 cars & buses, 1000 passengers.

Black Ball Transport Inc.--430 Belleville Street, Victoria V8V 1W9, Victoria: (604) 386-2202, Port Angeles: (206) 457-4491

Goes to: Port Angeles, Olympic Peninsula, Washington to Victoria, B.C. 1 hr 35 min, 100 cars, 800 passengers. On busy days with overflow travelers, you may find yourself stranded in Port Angeles with no choice but to stay with your vehicle overnight or leave and lose your place in line. Prepare for this possibility when making travel plans.

Washington State Ferries--Washington State Dept. of Transportation, Marine Division, Colman Dock, Seattle, WA 98104 or 2499 Ocean Ave., Sidney, B.C. V8L 1T3

Seattle: (800) 542-7052, (206) 464-6400

Victoria: (604) 381-1551

Sidney: (604) 656-1531

Goes to: Anacortes, WA (mainland) to Sidney, B.C. with San Juan Island stops, 3 hr, 160 cars, 2000 passengers. Daily departures, year round.

The trip through the San Juans is a scenic way to reach Vancouver Island. You may take your own car, or ride

Evergreen Trailways bus between Sidney and Victoria. Evergreen also operates buses from Seattle to Victoria on the international sailing. Call **Evergreen Trailways** in Seattle for schedules, fares, and reservations (206) 624-5077.

Note: On most ferries, vehicles including motor homes will be charged extra for each foot over 20 ft in length including trailer hitches. If you drive a long vehicle, practice backing, as you may have to getting on or off ferries. Observe ferry safety requirements for vehicles, passengers, and pets, including non-smoking and fuel container regulations. For RV-drivers, the Travel Infocentres have lists of sani-station facilities offered at many private campgrounds and businesses in each town on the Island.

Train Travel

VIA Rail offers service between Prince Rupert, Prince George, and points east and south. Going east, the train crosses the Canadian Rockies. From Prince George the train to Vancouver follows the Fraser River gorge. VIA also operates passenger-only daily service from Victoria to Courtenay, the scenic "Malahat Railiner" on Vancouver Island, a **very** popular trip. Design your own 1-day excursions to see the east coast. Eat at local stops or bring your own lunch. Air conditioned cars. For best views, sit on sea side going north and south. Call (800) 665-8630. In Victoria, call (604) 383-4324.

Traveling by Air

For private pilots, airport customs entry points are open 8:30 am-4:30 pm at Campbell River, Courtenay, and Port Alberni, with 24 hr service at Nanaimo, Port Hardy, and Victoria airports. The British Columbia Aviation Council (604) 278-4160 distributes the Ministry of Transportation and Highways Air Facilities Map, giving information on 374 land & water airports on Vancouver Island and mainland B.C.

Many commercial airlines provide direct service from major U.S. and Canadian cities to Seattle, WA, and Vancouver, B.C. From Seattle and Vancouver, many connecting flights serve the Vancouver Island cities of Victoria, Nanaimo, Comox, Campbell River, and Port Hardy.

Canadian Airlines International - (800) 426-7000 or from WA State (800) 552-7576

San Juan Air - (206) 622-6077

The above airlines fly from SeaTac Airport near Seattle to Victoria.

Air B.C. - (800) 663-0522

Pacific Western Airlines - (604) 684-6161

Burrard Air - (604) 278-7178

For information about other airlines serving Vancouver Island, including west coast fixed wing and helicopter services, contact the Tourism Association of Vancouver Island.

Fly-in glass ball beach, west coast Vancouver Island.

Bus Tours & Travel

Intercity, modern, air-conditioned coaches regularly travel the major ferry routes--a simple and economical way to travel to the Island. On the Victoria, Vancouver, Nanaimo, Sunshine

Coast routes, you can travel on regularly scheduled bus services, downtown to downtown. Your luggage stays on the coach when it boards the ferry and there are lots of convenient pick-up and drop-off places en route. Once on Vancouver Island, you can connect easily by highway bus with Port Hardy--the ferry terminal for the Inside Passage route--and with all the major Island communities. From Vancouver, scheduled services link with all North American communities.

Call: **Island Coach Lines Ltd.**, 710 Douglas St., Victoria, B.C. V8W 2B3 (604) 385-4411

Greyhound Lines, 150 Dunsmuir St., Vancouver, B.C. V6B 1W9 (604) 662-3222.

City buses on Vancouver Island link with intercity coaches traveling the major ferry routes. Contact the **Victoria Regional Transit System** (604) 382-6161 (bus depot behind the Empress Hotel corner of Douglas & Belleville Sts.) or **Gray Line Victoria** (604) 388-5248/(800) 663-8390 for sightseeing, leaves in front of the Empress Hotel.

Driving

Buckle Up. It's B.C. law. You are also responsible for properly restraining children and infants in your vehicle. Infants less than 9 kg or 20 lbs must sit in an infant restraint. Children between 20-40 lbs must have a toddler restraint. Children over 6 years or 40 lbs must ride buckled into adult seatbelts.

Don't Drink & Drive. A blood alcohol count of .08% is legally drunk and applies to operators of boats and planes as well as cars.

Rental cars are available in Victoria, Nanaimo, and all major towns on Vancouver Island.

If you get in a traffic accident in British Columbia, call the Insurance Corporation of British Columbia [in Victoria (604) 383-1111] for claims advice. For general information: (604) 661-2800. U.S. motorists should get a Canadian non-resident Interprovince motor-vehicle liability in-surance card from their own insurance company.

Nanaimo Harbour.

Kayak camp, Broken Group, Barkley Sound -- Pacific Rim National Park.

Customs

U.S. citizens must have identification, even for infants. All other visitors to Canada must have a valid national passport or other recog-nized travel documents. You may be required to show enough money for your trip through Canada, at least $150.

U.S. residents returning from Canada after more than 48 hrs may take back free of duty $400 worth of articles for personal or household use. If less than 48 hrs, you may bring back articles free of duty and tax worth $25.

Revolvers, pistols and fully automatic firearms are prohibited.

Dogs and cats from the U.S. must have a certificate signed by a veterinarian of Canada or the U.S. certifying vaccination against rabies during the preceding 36 months, with a legible description of the animal and vaccination date.

Fresh fruit or plants crossing the border in either direction may be impounded to prevent transport of diseases or pests.

For other border crossing information, contact the Tourism Association of Vancouver Island or the Canadian consulate in your own country.

Money

The Canadian money system is based on dollars and cents, making the conversion easy for U.S. citizens. Exchange your funds for Canadian dollars at a bank or a foreign currency exchange outlet, where you will get the prevailing rate of exchange.

Metric System

Canada operates on the international metric system of weights and measures: kilometers (mileage), litres (pumping gasoline & buying beverages), kilograms or "kilos & tonnes" (weights), and Celsius (temperature). For conversion tables, consult travel centres, any dictionary, or your local library.

Pets

If you plan to spend time in the backcountry or on the water during your visit to Vancouver Island, I suggest you leave your pets at home under responsible care. A dog or cat does not belong on a salmon fishing or whale watching boat where he can disturb others or have trouble relieving himself. Pets taken into the backcountry can disturb wildlife even though you don't realize what is happening. And no pet deserves to be shut up alone in an RV while you go off sightseeing. Finding accommodations will be much easier without an animal along. Give your pet a holiday away from you!

Photography

The challenge of photography on Vancouver Island, like most of the Pacific Northwest, is trying to get **action** at a **distance** in **low light**. It is incredibly hard to photograph whales from a moving boat, on a gray day, not knowing when or where they might surface. Autofocus cameras really don't help here or with most other active wildlife since the mechanism stays just a few fractions of a second behind the action. Your best bet is to practice and get good at follow-focusing. Shoot the highest speed film that will still do the job for you after development. Use the "fastest" lenses you can afford.

The other major problem is **moisture**--humidity and water immersion. Salt water spells death to cameras. For diving, you can buy waterproof bags for SLR cameras. It's probably better to rent or buy a true underwater camera for serious photography. If you will be traveling for longer than 2 weeks in wet country, a sealed dry box with desiccant for exposed film and your lenses is important.

Port Alberni Harbour Quay.

17. HOTELS, CAMPING, SPECIAL RESTAURANTS

Vancouver Island has hundreds of good hotels, motels, bed-and-breakfasts, sport fishing camps and lodges (including fly-in or boat-in) plus hundreds more campgrounds, for both tents and recreational vehicles, in public parks (national, provincial, regional and urban), private parks and on crown (public) lands-- all at prices that compare favorably with those in the U.S. and Europe. Every year since 1925, the B.C. Ministry of Tourism, Recreation and Culture has published a comprehensive **Accommodations Guide** and distributed thousands of copies free. You can get a current copy of this guide by contacting: Ministry of Tourism, Recreation and Culture, 1117 Wharf Street, Victoria, B.C. V8W 2Z2; or Tourism Association of Vancouver Island (Ch16), (604) 382-3551. The **Guide** is also available at Travel Infocentres (Ch16) on the Island. The Tourism Association, the marketing branch of the Ministry of Tourism, publishes a list of its members as well.

It's nearly impossible for the **Traveler** to list all the available accommodations on the Island. However, it is important that you book space well ahead if you plan to travel in the busy season, May to September, or on holiday weekends. Federal and provincial campgrounds do not take reservations. Write the parks (Ch19) for information. Some RV parks and campgrounds do take reservations. Inclusion in the Ministry's **Guide** does not imply recent inspection or approval from the B.C. Ministry of Tourism. However, if you have complaints or compliments about service from any of the accommodations listed, you should contact the Ministry of Tourism or the Tourism Association promptly.

The following list introduces you to Island accommodations. Use price ranges (in $Can) as a guide only; contact each establishment for exact prices. Nights are cool, so air conditioning usually isn't needed on Vancouver Island. The best accommodations on the west coast and North Island will go fast during busy season, so book reservations **early**.

Hostels

Canadian Hostelling Association, Regional Office, 3425 West Broadway, Vancouver, B.C. V6R 2B4 (604) 736-2674

Elderhostel, 80 Boylston St. Suite 400, Boston, MA 03116

Victoria Hostel, 516 Yates St., Victoria, B.C. V8W 1K8 (604) 385-5313. Also note the **Pack & Boots Shop** at the same address and phone for current information on hostels and mini-hostels open on Vancouver Island.

Bed & Breakfasts

Accommodations West B&B Reservation Service, P.O. Box 6161, Station C, Victoria, B.C. 479-1986

All Seasons B&B Agency, Box 5511, Station B, Victoria, B.C. V8R 6S4 (604) 595-2337

City & Sea B&B Agency, #126--790 Topaz Ave., Victoria, B.C. V8T 2M1 (604) 385-1962

Garden City B&B Reservation Service, P.O. Box 6398, Station C, Victoria, B.C. V8P 5N7 (604) 479-9999

Hosts of the South West Coast B&B, Vancouver Island, RR#4, Sooke, B.C. V0S 1N0 (604) 642-6534

Hotels, Motels, & Campgrounds (Tent & RV)

Listed in alphabetical order by towns.

Key:

$15-25, $25-50, etc.--Price for single party, add $10-20 per extra person. Rates are in $CAN.

Resv--Reservations recommended/required. Check with each hotel or campground for their cancellation policy.

Hot/Jaq/Pool--Hot tub, swirl pool, swimming pool.

JR/SR Rate--Special rates for children/senior citizens.

TV--Television may be cable or satellite.

Kit--Full kitchen.

Share bath--Shared vs private bathroom facilities.

DD--Direct dial phone.

P--Pets acceptable.

CR--Commissionable rates for travel agents.

WA--Wheelchair accessibility.

¥ or ¥¥--Partial or full hookups available.

Tent/RV--Tent camping or recreational vehicles.

Alert Bay

Old Depot Cottage, Box 483, Alert Bay, B.C. V0N 1A0 (604) 674-5974. Kit, TV, $50-100.

Campground:

Oceanview Camping & Trailer Park, P.O. Box 28, Alert Bay, B.C. V0N 1A0 (604) 974-5213. Great view overlooking Johnstone Strait, ¥¥, BBQ's, nature trails, ferry dock, free boat launch, golf course adjacent, can explore whole island on foot, recommended, $15-25.

Bamfield

Aguilar House, Bamfield, B.C. V0R 1BO (604) 728-3323. Lodges & cottages on the Pacific Ocean, family-style meals, adventure packages, group rates, min 2-day stay, Resv, P, $75-100.

Bamfield Trails Motel, Box 7, Bamfield, B.C. V0R 1B0 (604) 728-3231. Bamfield Inlet overlook, TV, laundry, Pool, Hot, Jaq, fish & hike, $35-75.

Campground:

Poett Nook Campground & Marina c/o 2178 Camelon Dr., Port Alberni, B.C. V9Y 1B2 (604) 723-7930. Camp, 20 km N. of Bamfield, ¥¥, hot showers, firewood, shaded & sunny sites, $11-20.

Campbell River

Anchor Inn, 261 Island Hwy, Campbell River, B.C. V9W 2B3 (604) 286-1131. Balconies overlook the water, driftfishing with the tide, excellent licensed dining & bar, Hot/Jaq/Pool, TV, DD, WA, charters & boat rentals available, friendly staff, recommended, $75-100.

April Point Lodge & Fishing Resort, Box 1, Campbell River, B.C. V9W 4Z9 (604) 285-2222. Island resort with beautiful seafront guest houses & suites, licensed dining, Hot, Jaq, Pool, marina, WA, P, CR, Family plans, $100-150.

Bachmairs Bavarian Apart-Hotel, 492 S. Island Hwy, Campbell River, B.C. V9W 1A5 (604) 923-2848. Discovery Passage overlook, balconied suites, Kit, TV, nice atmosphere, $65-100.

Friendship Inn Motel & RV Park, 3900 North Island Hwy, Campbell River, B.C. V9W 2J2 (604) 287-9591. Motel, Camp, TV, DD, WA, ¥¥, laundromat, store, $12-50.

Marina Inn Resort, 1430 South Island Hwy, Campbell River, B.C. V9W 5T7 (604) 923-7255. Overlooks Discovery Passage, DD, TV, licensed dining & pub, fishing guides, family plan, recommended, $50-75.

Passage View, 517 Island Hwy, Campbell, River, B.C. V9W 2B9 (604) 286-1156. Beach access, all rooms view of Discovery Passage & Quadra Island, close to shopping & salmon fishing, Kt, DD, TV, airport limo service, CR, $40-60.

Quadra Resort, Box 175, Quathiaski Cove, B.C. V0P 1N0 (604) 285-3279. Gowlland Harbour secluded guest houses with fine views, Kit, WA, freezer, boat & canoe rentals, moorage, guides, weekly & off season rates, Resv, $55-75.

Seascape Waterfront Resort, Box 92, Campbell River, B.C. V9W 4Z9 (604) 285-3450. Secluded waterfront cottages at Gowlland Harbour, Kit with patio decks, laundry, guided fishing, moorage & rentals, hiking, clamming, oysters, P, weekly & off season rates, $50-75.

Super 8 Motel, 340 South Island Hwy, Campbell River, B.C. V9W 1A5 (604) 286-6622, (800) 843-1991. Water beds, some WA, TV, DD, airport 8 km, SR Rate, suites, non-smoking rooms, $50-75.

Campground: see **Friendship Inn.**

Comox

The Alders Beach Resort, P.O. Box 2, Merville, B.C. V0R 2M0 (604) 337-5322. Quiet condo cottages on 274 m of sandy beach with spacious ground, laundry, shellfish & salmon fishing in area, recommended, CR, $75-100.

Miracle Beach Resort, RR1, Black Creek, B.C. V0R 1C0 (604) 337-5171. Cottages on beach, Kit, ¥¥, sani-station, showers, laundry, store, freezer, fishing & boat rentals, fuel, cottages $50-55, camp-sites $10-20.

Port Augusta Motel, 2082 Comox Ave., Comox, B.C. V9N 4A7 (604) 339-2277. View of Comox Bay, licensed dining & pub, some waterbeds, DD, TV, P, fishing charters, nearby skiing, golf, tennis & beaches, 8 km from Powell River-Comox Ferry & airport, CR, $35-55.

Campgrounds:

Bates Beach Boathouse & RV Park, Bates Beach, RR 2, Courtenay, B.C. V9N 5M9 (604) 334-4154. On the ocean, Kit, ¥¥, flush toilets, showers, laundry, boat rentals, freezer, launch, shellfish, cottages $25-55, campsites $12-15.

Also see: **Miracle Beach Resort.**

Courtenay

Anco Slumber Lodge, 1885 Cliffe Ave., Courtenay, B.C. V9N 2K9 (604) 334-2451. Resv, Kit, DD, TV, Hot-Pool, coffee shop, WA, P, CR, $30-45.

Arbutus Travelodge, 275 8th St., Courtenay, B.C. V9N 1N4 (604) 334-3121, (800) 255-3050. Off Island Hwy, licensed dining & pub with entertainment, waterbeds, coffee shop, DD, TV, P, conferences, ski & fishing packages, CR, $40-55.

Collingwood Inn, 1675 Cliffe Ave., Courtenay, B.C. V9N 2K6 (604) 338-1464. Downtown, Kit, DD, TV, laundry, licensed dining & pub, family rates, WA, P, CR, $40-60.

Economy Inns Ltd., 2605 Cliffe Ave., Island Hwy, Courtenay, B.C. V9N 2L8 (604) 334-4491. Near hwy but quiet, TV, Hot Pool, access fishing & ski areas, P, CR, $30-40.

The Kingfisher Inn, RR 3, 4330 S. Island Hwy, Courtenay, B.C. V9N 5M8 (604) 338-1323. On the ocean, Hot-Jaq-Pool, tennis, waterfront, licensed dining & pub, conferences, ski & fishing packages, recommended, RV sites, boat launch, off season rates, CR, hotel $45-65, sites $7-10.

River Heights Motel, 1820 Cliffe Ave., Courtenay, B.C. V9N 2K8 (604) 338-8932. Quiet, Kt, TV, WA, P, CR, $30-55.

Sleepy Hollow Inn, 1190 CLiffe Ave., Island Hwy 19, Courtenay, B.C. V9N 2K1 (604) 334-4476. Downtown, Kit, TV, DD, WA, P, non-smoking rooms, Jaq-Pool, fitness centre, conferences, CR, $35-50.

The Washington Inn, 1001 Ryan Rd., Courtenay, B.C. V9N 3R6 (604) 338-5441. View units, Jaq-Pool, DD, TV, licensed dining & pub, conferences, P, CR, $45-65.

The Westerly, 1590 Cliffe Ave., Courtenay, B.C. V9N 2K4 (604) 338-7741. River views, full service hotel, Hot-Jaq-Pool, licensed dining & pub, TV, WA, conventions, central for skiing & fishing, CR, $60-85.

Campgrounds: see **Kingfisher Inn**

Gold River

Coast Gold River Chalet, Box 10, Gold River, B.C. V0P 1G0 (604) 283-2244. Full service hotel, DD, TV, Pool, Resv, Off season rates $65-100.

Peppercorn Trail Motel & RV Park, Box 23, Gold River, B.C. V0P 1G0 (604) 283-2443. Motel, Camp, laundry, Sr Rate, ¥¥, TV Resv, $30-50.

Campgrounds: see **Peppercorn Trail Motel & RV Park**.

Nanaimo

Best Western Harborview Motor Inn, 809 Island Hwy South, RR 1, Nanaimo, B.C. V9R 5K1 (604) 754 8171. Jaq/Pool, non-smoking rooms, TV, WA, in-room movies, family restaurant, conventions, laundry, Kit, $55-75.

Bluebird Motel, 995 North Terminal Ave., Nanaimo, B.C. V9S 4K3 (604) 753-4151. Close to shops, golf, fishing, TV, DD, P, WA, Kit, CR, $40-55.

Coast Bastion Inn, 11 Bastion Street, Nanaimo, B.C. V9R 2A9 U.S. & Canada: (800) 663-1144 High quality with excellent views. SR rates. $70-over 100.

Other Coast Hotels: **Coast Discover Inn**, Campbell River; **Coast Gold River Chalet**, Gold River; **Coast Tahsis Chalet**, Tahsis; **Coast Chateau Victoria**, Victoria; **Coast Harbour Towers**, Victoria

Departure Bay Motel, 2011 Estevan Rd. & Island Hwy, N. Nanaimo, B.C.V9S 3Y9 (604) 754-2161. Kit, TV, WA, P, DD, CR, $45-55.

Highlander Motor Inn, 96 North Terminal Ave., Nanaimo, B.C. V9S 4J2 (604) 754-6355. Jct Hwys 1 & 19 from ferries, TV, WA, P, patios, restaurant nearby, complimentary continental breakfast, CR, $50-75.

Moby Dick Boatel, 1000 Stewart Ave., Nanaimo, B.C. V9S 4C9 (604) 753-7111. Seaside with marina facilities & free canoeing, balconies view ocean, WA, elevator, TV, Kit, P, laundry, charters arranged, CR, $35-55.

Northgate Motor Inn, 6450 Metral Dr., Nanaimo, B.C. V9T 2L8 (604) 390-2222. Hwy 19 @ Woodgrove Shopping Centre, Jaq, licensed dining. Near golf, TV DD, WA, CR, $45-65.

Port-O-Call Motel, 505 Terminal Ave., North Nanaimo, B.C. V9S 4K1 (604) 753-3421. Near ferries, hospital, golf courses, Kit, WA, TV, DD, 24-hr. customer service, Pool, exercise room, SR Rates CR, $35-55.

The Royal Motel, 335 North Terminal Ave., Nanaimo, B.C. V9S 4J6 (604) 753-1171. Close to shops, restaurants, ferries, connecting units, TV, DD, laundry, Kit, CR, $35-50.

Schooner Cove Resort Complex, Box 12 Schooner House, Nanoose Bay, B.C. V0R 2R0 (604) 468-7691. Hotel & condos, many with ocean view, licensed dining, WA, Hot-Jaq-Pool, exercise room & tennis courts, conventions, store, marina, moorage, boat rentals, charters, CR, $75-100.

Tally-Ho Island Inns, 1 Terminal Ave., Nanaimo, B.C. V9R 5R4 (604) 753-2241, (800) 663-7322. Sea view downtown, licensed dining & pub, Hot Pool outdoors, conventions, DD, TV, CR, $50-75.

Westward Ho Motel, 250 Terminal Ave., North Nanaimo, B.C. V9S 4J5 (604) 754-4202. Near ferries, private patio, Pool, Kit, TV, DD, P, CR $40-65.

Westwood Lake RV Camping & Cabins, Site D, RR3, Nanaimo, B.C. V9R 5K3 (604) 753-3922. Treed grounds near lake fishing & nature trails, ¥¥, showers, laundry, store, boat rentals, CR, Via Comox/Bowen Rd., left at Wakesiah Rd., to Jingle Pot Rd. then left at Westwood Lk. Park Rd., Cabins $40-50, Campsites $10-15.

Campgrounds: see above and

Beban Park Regional District Campground, 2300 Bowen Rd., Nanaimo, B.C. V9T 3K7 (604) 758-1177. W. of Hwy 19 on Bowen Road, part of recreation complex with swimming, skating, sauna, tennis & cultural activities avail. extra cost, flush toilets, showers, fire pits, $7-10.

Jingle Pot Campsite, RR3, Site K, 4012 Jingle Pot Rd., Nanaimo, B.C. V9R 5K3 (604) 758-1614. Quiet, shaded campsites off hwy 8 km N. of Nanaimo, ¥¥, washrooms, sani-station, store, ice, fishing charters, CR, $10-15.

Seabreeze Mobile Home Park, RR1, Maki Road, Nanaimo, B.C. V9R 5K1 (604) 754-6481. Campground 3 km S. of city center, RV & trailer sites, ¥¥, flush toilets, showers, laundry, CR, $10-15.

Parksville

The Bayside Inn, 240 Dogwood St., Box 1690, Parksville, B.C. V0R 2S0 (604) 248-8333, (800) 663-4232. Off hwy on sandy Parksville Bay. Ocean & mountain views, licensed dining & pub, Hot-Jaq-Pool, aerobics room, tennis, racquetball, squash, shops, con-ferences, recommended, CR, Resv, $85-115.

Bloomfield Motel, 411 W. Island Hwy, Box 2189, Parksville, B.C. V0R 2S0 (604) 248-6171. Near beach, restaurants & fishing. Some suites, Kit & waterbeds, off-season rates, P, CR, $25-55.

Cameron Lake Resort, RR2, Qualicum Beach, B.C. V0R 2T0 (604) 752-6707. Apr-Oct cottages on Cameron Lake, 20 km west of Parksville on Hwy 4, sandy beach, Kit, laundry, store, boat & canoe rentals, launching, hiking, fishing, fire pits, CR, P, $40-50.

French Creek Campground & Cottages, RR 3, Site 317, C-73, Parksville, B.C. V0R 2S0 (604) 248-3998. Quiet, off hwy, private cottages most with fireplaces, TV, Hot-Jaq-Pool, racquet ball court, fitness room, off season rates, treed park setting campground, showers, flush toilets, laundry, licensed dining & pub on ocean, store, near government launch & moorage with fuel, recom-mended, cottages $65-110, campsites $9-15.

Friendship Inn Fireside Motel, Box 562, 272 W. Island Hwy, Parksville, B.C. V0R 2S0 (604) 248-4261. Near beach & downtown, Hot Pool with service. Licensed dining & pub, outdoor dining, TV, Kit, fishing charter, CR, $25-90.

Tigh Na Mara, RR#1, Site 114, C16, Parksville, B.C. V0R 2S0 (604) 248-2072. Log cottages tucked in woods by the sea, wood burning fireplaces & electric heat, balcony rooms with great view across ocean, Hot, Pool, RV,¥¥,CR,P,WA, off season rates, $75-over 100.

Campgrounds: see **French Creek Campground & Cottages.**

Port Alberni

Timber Lodge Motor Inn, Port Alberni Hwy, Port Alberni, B.C. V9Y 7L6 (604) 723-9415. Motor hotel, TV, DD, movies, Hot, Pool, Licensed dining, breakfast with room, $50-75.

Campgrounds:

Dry Creek Park Public Campground, City Hall, 4850 Argyle St., Port Alberni, B.C. V9Y 1V8 (604) 723-6011. Camp May-Sep, beside creek, ¥¥, $8-15.

Junction Service Campground, RR2, Site 215, C-6, Port Alberni, B.C. V9Y 7L6 (604) 723-2606.Camp Apr-Oct, near Infocentre, ¥¥, laundromat, store, $10-20.

Port Alice

Quatsino Chalet, Box 280, Port Alice, B.C. V0N 2N0 (604)284-3318. On Neroutsos Inlet. Hskpg units available, TV, Pool, licensed dining, fishing charters, Resv, CR, $50-75.

Port Hardy

Best Western Port Hardy Inn, Box 1798, Port Hardy, B.C. V0N 2P0 (604) 949-8525. 9040 Granville St., central location, harbor view, TV, DD, Pool, dining, CR, WA, P, full service hotel, $62-75.

Eagle Manor Retreat, Box 72, Coal Harbour, B.C. V0N 1K0 (604) 949-7895. Take private boat or mail ferry to Quatsino. Fine place to relax overlooking sound on 15 ac, WA, P, Resv, speak German too, $about 50.

Glen Lyon Inn, Box 103, Port Hardy, B.C. V0N 2P0 (604) 949-7115. 6435 Hardy Bay Rd, full view of Hardy Bay, TV, DD, boat launch, licensed dining, Resv, $50-75.

God's Pocket Resort, Box 471, Port Hardy, B.C. V0N 2P0 (604) 733-5828.Dive and fishing packages, beautiful bay view, nature walks, meals in cookhouse, Resv, $50-75.

The North Shore Inn, 7370 Market St., Box 1888, Port Hardy, B.C. V0N 2P0 (604) 949-8500. 39 Hardy Bay view rooms, licensed dining with live entertainment, charter boats & diving packages, CR, $50-75.

Port Hardy Airport Inn, Box 2039 Airport Rd, Port Hardy, B.C. V0N 2P0 (604) 949-9434. Off Hwy near airport, Kit, TV, DD, Resv, $30-50.

Seagate Hotel, Box 28, Port Hardy, B.C. V0N 2P0 (604) 949-6348. Spacious view rooms with 700 feet of ocean front, downtown, licensed dining & pub, live entertainment conference rooms, Kit, fishing charters, Resv, 2nd day stay packages, $25-55.

Thunderbird Inn, Rupert & Granville, Box 88, Port Hardy, B.C. V0N 2P0 (604) 949-7767. Central location for shopping & sight-seeing, limo service, licensed dining & pub, live entertainment, DD, TV, fishing & diving charters, CR, tour packages, $50-75.

Campgrounds:

Quarterdeck Marina, Box 910, Port Hardy, B.C. V0N 2P0 (604) 949-6551. Marina & RV Park, ¥¥, tackle, bait, boats & charters, moorage with power & fuel, marine repairs, laundry, shower, ice, launch ramp, Resv, weekly & monthly rates, closed Sunday, $15-25.

Quatse River Campsite, Box 1350, Port Hardy, B.C. V0N 2P0 (604) 949-8233. Old Island Highway across from Pioneer Inn, 4 km from Port Hardy, 8 km from Prince Rupert ferry, trees by river, showers, laundry, flush/dry toilets, free firewood, 60 campsites, 23 with water & electricity, $10-15.

Wildwoods Campsite, Box 801, Port Hardy, B.C. V0N 2P0 (604) 949-6753. Camp, on road to Prince Rupert ferry, firewood, beach access & boat moorage, P, $10-20.

Sunny Sanctuary Campground, Box 552, Port Hardy, B.C. V0N 2P0 (604) 949-8111. Camp, on ferry route, near wildlife sanctuary, ¥¥, public phone, weekly & monthly rates, $10-20.

Qualicum Beach

Ben Bow Inn, Box 1642, Qualicum Beach, B.C. V0R 2T0 (604) 752-5666. Near beach, rooms & townhouse suites, TV, Pool & Jaq, DD, Kit, off season rates, CR, $60-90.

Best Western College Inn, Box 99, Qualicum Beach, B.C. V0R 2T0 (604) 752-9262. Full service hotel on 4 acres with ocean view & beach access, licensed dining & pub with entertainment, Hot-Jaq-Pool, conferences, honeymoon suite, CR, $50-100.

The Crescent Resort Hotel, 431 W. Crescent Rd., Qualicum Beach, B.C. V0R 2T0 (604) 752-9551. On high bluff off hwy overlooking ocean, 9-hole putting green, shuffleboard, quiet & secluded, TV, week rates, Resv, CR, $45-55.

Ocean Beach Resort, P.O. Box 52, McFeely Rd., Qualicum Beach, B.C. V0R 2T0 (604) 752-9322. McFeely Rd. off Island Hwy, turn at Kinkade Rd. approx. 500 m, sandy beach, ocean front, Kit, TV, ¥¥, laundry, fishing charters, family plan, WA, cottages $400 per week, campground $15-20.

Riverside Resort, Box 1859, Qualicum Beach, B.C. V0R 2T0 (604) 752-9544. Sandy ocean beach & park-like setting on 7 acres by Little Qualicum River, Hot Pool, ¥¥, showers, laundry, store, TV, Kit, playground, fishing, P, cottages $30-45, campsites $10-15.

Sand Pebbles Inn, Box 145, Qualicum Beach, B.C. V0R 2T0 (604) 752-6974. Motel on the beach, licensed dining, TV, conferences, indoor racquet ball court, golf, tennis nearby, CR, $55-75.

The Shorewater Motel, 3295 W. Island Hwy., Qualicum Beach, B.C. V0R 2T0 (604) 752-6901. Family units on beach, landscaped grounds, Kit, TV, DD, laundry, off season rates, P, CR, $55-75.

Campgrounds:

Cedar Grove Tent & Trailer Park, RR 1, Comp. 19, Qualicum Beach, B.C. V0R 2T0 (604) 752-2442. Fishing on Little Qualicum River, ¥¥, sani-station, flush toilets, showers, laundry, store, grassy campsites, fires, swimming, playground, tables, nearby golf, shops, week & month rates, $10-15.

Costa Lotta Campground, RR 3, Site 324, C-15, Qualicum Beach, B.C. V0R 2T0 (604) 757-8483. Beachfront 11 km N. of Qualicum Beach, ¥¥, sani-station, showers, laundry, store, shaded sites, large community shelter, fishing, boat rentals, cement launch, charters & guides, beach firepits, play area, $10-15.

Qualicum Beach Trailer Park, Box 1706, Qualicum Beach, B.C. V0R 2T0 (604) 752-2324. Near beach, N. of Qualicum, ¥¥, sami-station, TV, laundry, dry storage avail., pay phones, picnic tables, $15-20.

Roll'n Homes Campground, Site 119-C6, RR 1, Bennett Rd., Qualicum Beach, B.C. V0R 2T0, (604) 752-6816. Campground 8 km N. of Parksville on Airport Rd., trees & playground, ¥¥, showers, flush toilets, exercise room, laundry, sani-station, near golf course, charter fishing, Resv, $10-15.

Also see: **Ocean Beach Resort** and **Riverside Resort**.

Sayward

Fisherboy Park, Sayward, B.C. V0P 1R0 (604) 282-3204. Ideal half-way stop to Prince Rupert Ferry leaving from Port Hardy, 45 shaded sites by the Salmon River, WA, P,¥¥, Tent/RV, $10-25.

RV and tent camping at Sayward near Oscar.

Sidney

Emerald Isle Motor Inn, 2306 Beacon Ave., Sidney, B.C. V8L 1X2 (604) 656-4441. For reservations, call collect. Walking distance to entire town, large comfortable units, Kit, TV & movies, laundromat, WA,CR,DD, off season rates,$50-75.

Sointula

Beachcombers Inn, Box 380, Sointula, B.C. V0N 3E0 (604) 973-6366. Hotel retreat on Malcolm Island, settled and farmed by Finns, on Broughton Strait, day or weekly rates, $50-75.

Sooke

Malahat Farm, Anderson Rd., RR2, Sooke, B.C. V0S 1N0 (604) 642-6868. 14 km west of Sooke, heritage house of 1896, 45 acres of privacy & peace with full farm breakfast, near beachcombing & surfing, hiking & birdwatching, fishing charters, $80-100.

Point-No-Point Resort, RR2, Sooke, B.C. V0S 1N0 (604) 646-2020. Resv, fireplaces, Kit, fishing charters & kayak trips arranged, great 60 ac woods, beaches, coves, headlands, $50-75.

Point No Point Resort.

Sooke Harbour House, 1528 Whiffen Spit road, RR4, Sooke, B.C. V0S 1N0 (604) 642-3421. Resv, 37 km west of Victoria on Whiffen Spit Beach, ocean view rooms, Jaq & fireplaces, antique furnishings, excellent restaurant, some share bath, highly recommended, $50-over100.

Strathcona Park

Strathcona Park Lodge, Box 2160, Campbell River, B.C. V9W 5C9 (604) 286-2008. Resv, on Upper Campbell & Buttle Lakes system, lakefront chalets with balconies, some Kit, some share bath, full outdoor education resort for singles, groups, families, highly recommended, CR, P, $50-75.

Strathcona Park Lodge.

Telegraph Cove

Bauza Cove Campground & Marina, Telegraph Cove, B.C. V0N 3J0 (604) 928-3131. Camp, showers, laundromat, store, boat launch, guides, whale watch Johnstone Strait, Resv, WA, P, $10-25.

Tofino

Clayoquot Lodge, Box 188, Tofino, B.C. V0R 2Z0 (604) 725-3998. Resv, on Stubbs Island, 2 km by sea west of Tofino, Apr-Oct private island resort, 160 ac, beaches & rainforest, whale watching & fishing, boat pick-up from Tofino, $100-150.

Crystal Cove Resort, Box 559, Tofino, B.C. V0R 2Z0 (604) 725-4213. Log cottages on ocean, Kit & fireplaces, treed & beach

Schooner Cover, Pacific Rim National Park.

Tofino Swell Lodge.

campsites, ¥¥, showers, flush toilets, fishing & swimming, 3 km S. of Tofino, cottages $75-100, campsites $15-20.
Dolphin Motel, Box 116, Tofino, B.C. V0R 2Z0 (604) 725-3377. Near beach 3 km S. of Tofino, TV, Kit, $40-60.
Duffin Cove Motel, Box 178, Tofino, B.C. V0R 2Z0 (604) 725-3448. Up to 6 person units on ocean, fridges, barbecue, TV, near boating, beaches, store, dining, off season rates, P, $50-100.
Harbourview Units, 260 Main St., Box 41, Tofino, B.C. V0R 2Z0 (604) 725-3329. Tofino Harbour view in town center with deck, Kit, TV, barbecue, crab pot, charter boat, P, $50-75.
MacKenzie Beach Resort, Box 12, Tofino, B.C. V0R 2Z0 (604) 725-3439. Pacific ocean front, TV, Hot-Pool, ¥¥, P on lead in campground only, cottages $50-85, campsites $15-25.
Maquinna Hotel, Box 340, Tofino, B.C. V0R 2Z0 (604) 725-4434. Tofino Inlet overlook, licensed dining & pub, conferences, TV, CR, $40-70.
Mini Motel, Box 26, Tofino, B.C. V0R 2Z0 (604) 725-3441. Garden setting A-frames with views, Kit, TV, mini-resort, off season rates, Resv, cancel fee $10, $50-95.
Ocean Village Beach Resort, Box 490, Tofino, B.C. V0R 2Z0 (604) 725-3755. Gothic arch cottages with ocean view on MacKenzie Beach 3 km S. of Tofino, Kit, Hot-Jaq-Pool, near golf, store, laundry, conferences, cancel fee $7.50, Resv, CR, $70-100.
Pacific Sands Beach Resort, Box 237, Tofino, B.C. V0R 2Z0 (604) 725-3322. Facing ocean on Cox Bay with surfing & beachcombing, Kit, cottages with fireplaces, golf nearby, Resv, $55-95.
Schooner Motel, Box 202, Tofino, B.C. V0R 2Z0 (604) 725-3478. View, TV, $55-75.
Silver Cloud, Box 249, Tofino, B.C. V0R 2Z0 (604) 725-3998. Quiet lodge on lawn-lined beach, secluded with courtesy boat, "The Captain's Locker" full galley, bath & lounge, "The Eagles Nest" queen size bed on the water, full ensuite, double bed in the "Nook", twins in "Goldielocks", Resv, $80-150.
Tofino Swell Lodge, Box 160, Tofino, B.C. V0R 2Z0 (604) 725-3274. Resv, great view of Tofino inlet, shared Kit & lounge with outdoor BBQ, Hot Jaq, dock moorage, charter fishing, $50-75.

The Weigh West Motel, Box 553, 634 Campbell St., Tofino, B.C. V0R 2Z0 (604) 725-3277. Tofino Harbour central location, Kit, WA, TV, marine pub, nightly seafood barbecue in season, store, boat rentals & moorage, $25-85.

Campgrounds: see **Crystal Cove Resort** and **MacKenzie Beach Resort.**

Victoria

The Beaconsfield Inn, 998 Humboldt St., Victoria, B.C. V8V 2Z8 (604) 384-4044. Elegant English mansion on park & Inner Harbour, down comforters & some canopy beds, fireplaces, honeymoon suite, guest library & conservatory/sunroom, full breakfast included, recommended, CR, Resv, $75-175.

Captain's Palace, 309 Belleville St., Victoria, B.C. V8V 1X2 (604) 388-9191. Antique furnishings in 1897 hotel with hand-painted fresco ceilings, full complimentary breakfast with room, licensed dining overlooking harbor, conferences, recommended, CR, Resv, $65-150.

Craigflower Motel, 101 Island Hwy, Victoria, B.C. V9B 1E8 (604) 388-7861. On the Gorge waterway, good walking/bicycling, Kit, TV, laundromat, Hot pool, licensed dining, $50-75.

Empress Hotel, 721 Government St., Victoria, B.C. V8W 1W5 (604) 384-8111. Full service hotel that is a world famous institution, suites, licensed dining with entertainment, convention facilities to 500 people, family plans, special holiday packages & off season rates Oct-May, except Christmas, CR, $over 100.

Friendship Inn, 39 Gorge Road East, Victoria, B.C. V9A 1K7 (604) 386-8335. Right on the Gorge for scenic running & easy drive to downtown or airport, Kit suites, water beds, TV, licensed dining, P, truck/RV parking, ¥¥, DD, soundproof, rates Sept-June $25-50.

Harbour Towers, 345 Quebec St., Victoria, B.C. V8V 1W4 (604) 385-2405, Can/U.S.(800) 663-7555, B.C. (800) 742-6153. Full service near Parliament, Kit, DD, TV, Jaq-Hot-Pool, licensed dining & pub, gift shop, family plan, Resv. $100-175.

Huntington Manor Inn, 330 Quebec St., Victoria, B.C. V8W 1W3 (604) 381-3456, (800) 663-7557. Gallery bedroom suites, room service, central location, Jaq-Hot-Pool, TV, WA, laundry, covered parking, Resv, CR, $80-125.

Inn On The Harbour, 427 Belleville St., Victoria, B.C. V8V 1X3 (604) 386-3451. Ferries & Parliament nearby, TV, DD, Kit, licensed dining & pub, outdoor restaurant & pool in summer, CR, Resv, $55-100.

James Bay Inn, 270 Government St., Victoria, B.C. V8V 2L2 (604) 384-7151. Vicinity Parliament and Beacon Hill Park, TV, licensed dining, off season rates, CR, $25-50.

Oak Bay Beach Hotel, 1175 Beach Dr., Victoria, B.C. V8S 2N2 (604) 598-4556. Seaside, traditionally Victorian decor, TV, WA, Full service hotel with High Tea daily, American Plan available, Special packages arranged, highly recommended, $75-over 200.

The Royal Scot Motor Inn, 425 Quebec St., Victoria, B.C. V8V 1W7 (604) 388-5463. CR, near Parliament Bldgs, city center, TV, Pools, Hot, Jaq, Laundry, exercise room, recommended, $75-120.

Shamrock Motel, 675 Superior St., Victoria, B.C. V8V 1V1 (604) 385-8768. Family units with Kit, TV, DD, balcony, off season & SR rates, CR, Resv, $45-95.

Victoria Harbour House.

Surf Hotel, 290 Dallas Rd., Victoria, B.C. V8V 1A6 (604) 386-3305. Overlooking ocean with balconies, Kit, 5 blks S.

Parliament Bldgs, TV, WA, DD, $70-90.

University of Victoria B&B, P.O. Box 1700, Victoria, B.C. V8W 2Y2. Recreational facilities in park setting with easy access to Victoria, rates incl. breakfast, $15-30.

Victoria YWCA Hotel, 880 Courtney St., Victoria, B.C. V8W 1C4 (604) 386-7511. Central, shared bath, TV lounge, cafeteria, pool at rec. swim times, weekly rates Sept-May. $20-50.

Campgrounds: see Friendship Inn.

Yellowpoint

Inn Of The Sea Resorts, Yellow Point RD., RR 1, Ladysmith, B.C. V0R 2E0 (604) 245-2211. Seaview rooms & suites with balconies, Hot-Jaq-Pool, Kt, DD, TV, WA, licensed dining & pub, conventions, fishing, beachcombing, CR, $75-120.

Mermaid Cove Campground, RR 3, Ladysmith, B.C. V0R 2E0 (604) 245-3000. Jun-Sep, quiet seaside off hwy, Kit, fishing, clams, moorage, boat rentals, showers, Resv, cottages $30-40, campground $10-15.

Campgrounds: see above and

4 All Seasons Resort, RR 3, 3464 Yellow Point Rd., Ladysmith, B.C. V0R 2E0 (604) 245-4243. Campground on waterfront ¥¥, laundry, showers, club-house & arcade, Pool, store, fishing, boat ramp, guides, fuel, 3 day min. stay Jul-Aug, CR, $15-25.

The Zuiderzee Campsite, Yellow Point Rd., RR 3, Ladysmith, B.C. V0R 2E0 (604) 722-2334. Campground on Quennell Lake, Pool, showers, ¥¥, some cement pads, boats, launch, fishing, store, $10-15.

Special Restaurants

In addition to the restaurants mentioned as part of the accommodations listed here, I highly recommend you read *Island Treasures* by Carolyn Thomas & Jill Stewart for excellent restaurant choices and shopping information throughout Vancouver Island (Ch18.).

Undersea Gardens, Victoria.

Native Carvers in Bowl. (Verlie Burroughs)

18. GOOD READING

Here is much more than a standard bibliography. These are great reading in each field. I recommend them highly. If you have any titles you would like to see included in future editions of *Vancouver Island Traveler*, please contact me through Windham Bay Press.

Brewster, David, *British Columbia: Best Places*, Seattle, Washington: Sasquatch Books, 1985.

Brower, Kenneth, *The Starship and The Canoe*, New York: Harper & Row, Publishers, 1983.

Childerhose, R.J. and Trim, Marj, *Pacific Salmon*, Seattle, Washington: The University of Washington Press, 1981.

Cramond, Mike, *Vancouver Island Fishin' Holes*, Victoria, British Columbia: Pattison Ventures, Ltd., 1987.

Dowd, John, Sea Kayaking: *A Manual for Long-Distance Touring*, Vancouver, British Columbia: Douglas & McIntyre Ltd., 1986.

Duncan, Frances, and Harding, Rene, *Sayward: For Kelsey Bay*, Cloverdale, British Columbia: D.W. Friesen & Sons, 1979.

Dyson, George, *Baidarka,*, Edmonds, Washington: Alaska Northwest Publishing Co., 1986.

Ford, John and Deborah, "The Killer Whales of B.C.," Journal of the Vancouver Aquarium, Volume 5, Number 1, Summer 1981.

Garner, Joe, *Never Fly Over An Eagle's Nest*, Nanaimo, British Columbia: Cinnabar Press, 1982.

Haig-Brown, Roderick, *The Western Angler*, Don Mills, Ontario: Totem Books, 1981.

Hoyt, Erich, *Orca: The Whale Called Killer*, Camden East, Ontario: Camden House Publishing Ltd., 1984.

Reading

Ince, John, and Kottner, Hedi, *Sea Kayaking Canada's West Coast*, Vancouver, British Columbia: Raxas Books, Inc., 1982.

Kirkendall and Spring, *Bicycling the Pacific Coast*, Seattle, Washington: The Mountaineers, 1984.

Leadem, Tim, *The West Coast Trail*, Vancouver, British Columbia: Douglas & McIntyre Ltd., 1987.

Lillard, Charles, *Seven Shillings a Year: The History of Vancouver Island*, Ganges, British Columbia: Horsdal & Schubart Publishers Ltd., 1986.

McFeat, Tom, *Indians of The North Pacific Coast*, Ottawa, Canada: Carleton University Press, 1987.

McIntyre, J., ed., *Mind in The Waters*, New York: Charles Scribner's Sons, 1974.

Moe, Julia, *December Tide: Poems From Lighthouses, Inaccessible Islands, and Cabins in The Middle of Nowhere*, Madeira Park, British Columbia: Harbour Publishing, 1978.

Moe, Julia, *Eye of The Island*, Madeira Park, British Columbia: Harbour Publishing, 1982.

Obee, Bruce, *The Pacific Rim Explorer*, North Vancouver, British Columbia: Whitecap Books, 1986.

Obee, Bruce, *The Gulf Islands*, North Vancouver, British Columbia: Whitecap Books, 1981.

Outdoor Club of Victoria, *Hiking Trails I, II, III*, Victoria, British Columbia: Outdoor Club of Victoria, 1986.

Pattison, Ken, *Milestones on VAncouver Island*, Victoria, British Columbia: Pattison Ventures Ltd., 1986.

Peers, Elida, *101 Historical Buildings of The Sooke Region*, Sooke, British Columbia: Sooke Region Museum, 1985.

Peterson, Lester R., *The Cape Scott Story*, Vancouver, British Columbia: Mitchell Press, 1974.

Pratt-Johnson, Betty, *141 Dives in The Protected Waters of Washington & British Columbia*, Vancouver, British Columbia: Gordon Soules Economic and Marketing Research, 1976.

Pratt-Johnson, Betty, *Whitewater Trips for Kayakers, Canoeists & Rafters on Vancouver Island*, Vancouver, British Columbia: Gordon Soules Publishing, 1984.

Priest, Simon, and Klint, Kimberley, *Bicycling Vancouver Island and The Gulf Islands*, Vancouver, British Columbia: Douglas & McIntyre,1984.

Searby, Ellen, *Alaska's Inside Passage Traveler, See More / Spend Less!* Juneau, Alaska: Windham Bay Press, annually updated.

Sierra Club, *Victoria in a Knapsack*, Victoria, British Columbia: Sierra Club of Western Canada, 1985.

Stewart, Hilary, *Looking at Indian Art of The Northwest Coast*, Vancouver, British Columbia: Douglas & McIntyre Ltd., 1979.

Sutherland, Tom and Sandra, *Vancouver Island--A Colour Portrait*, West Vancouver, British Columbia: Sutherland Photo Productions, Inc., 1987.

Thomas, Carolyn, and Stewart, Jill, *Island Treasures*, Madeira Park, British Columbia: Harbour Publishing Co. Ltd., 1986.

Watmough, Don, *West Coast of Vancouver Island*, Vancouver, British Columbia: Maclean Hunter Ltd., 1984.

Weston, Jim, and Stirling, David, *The Naturalist's Guide to the Victoria Region*, Victoria, British Columbia: Victoria Natural History Society, 1986.

Woods, Erin and Bill, *Bicycling The Backroads of Northwest Washington & Backroads Around Puget Sound*, Seattle, Washington: The Mountaineers, 1984.

Thunderbird Park totem.

19. MAPS

To find/order maps, contact:

•BRITISH COLUMBIA AUTOMOBILE ASSOCIATION
999 West Broadway, Vancouver B.C. V5Z 1K5
(604) 732-3911
(Road maps)

•ISLAND BLUE PRINT, 905 Fort St, Victoria, B.C.
(604) 385-9786
(Map shop)

•METSKER MAPS OF TACOMA, 4020 So. Steele St.
Suite 107, Tacoma, WA 98409
(206) 474-MAPS
(Map shop)

•MINISTRY OF ENVIRONMENT & PARKS
PARKS & OUTDOOR RECREATION DIVISION
1610 Indian River Drive
North Vancouver, B.C. V7G 1L3
(604) 929-1291
(Vancouver Island PROVINCIAL PARKS map)

•MINISTRY OF TOURISM, RECREATION & CULTURE
1117 Wharf Street, Victoria, B.C. V8W 2Z2
(604) 387-1642
(Travel Planner, B.C. road maps, Accommodation Guide)

•PACIFIC RIM NATIONAL PARK
P.O. Box 280, Ucluelet, B.C. V0R 3A0
(604) 762-7721
(Park maps)

•REGIONAL DISTRICT OF MOUNT WADDINGTON
Box 729, Port McNeill, B.C. V0N 2R0
(604) 956-3301
(Maps of North Island & logging roads)

Maps

•TOURISM ASSOCIATION OF VANCOUVER ISLAND
302 - 45 Bastion Square, Victoria, B.C. V8W lJ1
(604) 382-3551
(Vancouver Island Marketing & Information Center)

•CANADIAN HYDROGRAPHIC SERVICE
Department of Fisheries and Oceans
P.O. Box 6000, Sidney, B.C. V8L 4B2
(604) 656-8358
(Canadian Nautical Charts and Tide Tables)

•CANADIAN HYDROGRAPHIC SERVICE
1675 Russell Road, Ottawa, Ontario K1G 3H6
(613) 993-0600
(Canadian Nautical Charts and Tide Tables)

SANDY BRYSON

Writer and photographer Sandy Bryson has written 3 books, produced video programs, and written outdoor articles for the San Francisco Chronicle-Examiner, Ford Times, City Sports, Climbing Magazine, and many others. She travels actively-- climbing Mt. Aconcagua on the Chile-Argentine border, backpacking in Tierra del Fuego, skiing in Switzerland, skindiving in Pacific Micronesia, and doing photography in Costa Rica. With search dogs she has trained, she has been on rescues throughout the Sierra and North American Rockies. Alpine County near Lake Tahoe is home base.

"The research trip for the Vancouver Island Traveler reinforced my affection for Canadians. Island resources are a great treasure. The living standard is high. I hope visitors will keep charging the economic batteries here to preserve the special qualities of this land and sea."

Index

20. INDEX

Index

FLASH! AS WE GO TO PRESS

The B. C. Summer Games will be held in Victoria, July 28-31, 1988. For more information write or call Summer and Winter Games, 777 Fort Street, Victoria, B. C. V8W 1G9. (604) 387-1375. The events will be fun, but be sure to have ferry and hotel reservations whether you plan to attend or not, if you will be on southern Vancouver Island during that time.

Notes

Notes

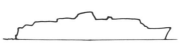

Books from Windham Bay Press, for the independent traveler:

Alaska's Inside Passage Traveler, See More/Spend Less, 11th edition by Ellen Searby. Photos, maps, 208 pages. Tells all you need to know to plan any kind of trip you want in the Inside Passage. This handy guide completely explains how to make the most of the Alaska ferry system, lists all the facilities in Southeast Alaska and Prince Rupert, B.C.with their prices, from deluxe hotels to cabins and youth hostels. Easy to read and use,with no paid advertising to weigh down your purse or pack. Enjoy a vacation according to your own interests on this beautiful coast. $9.95.ISBN 0-942297-01-6.

The Costa Rica Traveler, Getting Around in Costa Rica, 2nd edition, by Ellen Searby. Photos, maps, 256 pages. Peace, beauty, freedom. Enjoy this tropical Camelot with its friendly people, miles of uncrowded beaches, tropical rain forest, volcanoes, and jungle waterways. Visit the country that has 1/10th of the world's bird species, over 1200 species of orchids, altitudes from the Atlantic and Pacific Oceans to 12,600 feet, all in an area the size of West Virginia! Here is some of the world's best deep-sea fishing, snorkeling, river rafting—all at a reasonable cost. Hotels, facilities, and sights are clearly explained so you can make your choices. $11.95.ISBN 0-9605526-9-3.

Vancouver Island Traveler, Great Adventures on Canada's West Rim, by Sandy Bryson. Waters teeming with fish and whales, world-class diving and snow skiing, mild winters with green forests and lush golf courses right at the seashore, kayaking a wild west coast, board sailing fresh lake winds, bicycling into sunsets over Victoria harbor—where is all this water adventure with friendly people, easy to reach but still a priceless treasure? Canada's Vancouver Island, just a short ferry or plane ride west of Seattle and Vancouver. *Vancouver Island Traveler* gives you all the information you need to plan an exciting or relaxing getaway trip doing exactly what you like to do best.This unique guidebook shows you the Island through the eyes of experts who live there.The *Vancouver Island Traveler* takes you there! 208 pages, Photos, Maps. $10.95. ISBN 0-942297-00-8.

Windham Bay Press, Box 34283, Juneau, Alaska 99803

Number		Price	Amount
_____	*Alaska's Inside Passage Traveler*	$9.95	_____
_____	*Costa Rica Traveler*	$11.95	_____
_____	*Vancouver Island Traveler*	$10.95	_____

Postage & Handling: $_____
(U.S. surface $1 first book, .50 ea. add'l. Air, $2.50 first book, .50 ea.add'l.
Canada surface $1.50 first, $1 ea. add'l. Air, $3 first book, $1 ea. add'l.
Europe, Asia, Air $6.50 first book, $5 ea. add'l.)
Total payment enclosed $_____

Name_____

Address_____

City_____State/Prov._____

Zip_____ Country_____